Hurn
BARBECUE

RECIPES AND TECHNIQUES FROM A MASTER OF THE ART OF BBQ

Horn

BARBECUE

MATT HORN

HARVARD
COMMON
PRESS

Inspiring | Educating | Creating | Entertaining

Brimming with creative inspiration, how-to projects, and useful information to enrich your everyday life, Quarto.com is a favorite destination for those pursuing their interests and passions.

© 2022 Quarto Publishing Group USA Inc.
Text © 2022 Matt Horn
Photography © 2022 Andrew Thomas Lee

First Published in 2022 by The Harvard Common Press, an imprint of The Quarto Group,
100 Cummings Center, Suite 265-D, Beverly, MA 01915, USA.
T (978) 282-9590 F (978) 283-2742 Quarto.com

The Harvard Common Press titles are also available at discount for retail, wholesale, promotional, and bulk purchase. For details, contact the Special Sales Manager by email at specialsales@quarto.com or by mail at The Quarto Group, Attn: Special Sales Manager, 100 Cummings Center, Suite 265-D, Beverly, MA 01915, USA.

26 25 24 23 22   1 2 3 4 5

ISBN: 978-0-76037-426-9

Digital edition published in 2022
eISBN: 978-0-76037-427-6

Library of Congress Cataloging-in-Publication Data

Names: Horn, Matt, author.
Title: Horn barbecue : recipes and techniques from a master of the art
   of BBQ / Matt Horn.
Description: Beverly, MA, USA : Harvard Common Press, 2022. | Includes
   index. | Summary: "Matt Horn, the most celebrated new chef and pitmaster
   in the world of barbecue, reveals his smoke-cooking secrets in Horn
   Barbecue"-- Provided by publisher.
Identifiers: LCCN 2021051540 (print) | LCCN 2021051541 (ebook) | ISBN
   9780760374269 | ISBN 9780760374276 (eISBN)
Subjects: LCSH: Barbecuing. | LCGFT: Cookbooks.
Classification: LCC TX840.B3 H664 2022 (print) | LCC TX840.B3 (ebook) |
   DDC 641.5/78--dc23/eng/20211028
LC record available at https://lccn.loc.gov/2021051540
LC ebook record available at https://lccn.loc.gov/2021051541

Design: Cindy Samargia Laun
Photography by Andrew Thomas Lee except for images
on pages 19, 20, 25–31 and 221 courtesy of Matt Horn

Printed in China

DEDICATION

This book is dedicated to Nina, Matty, and Leilani, the loves of my life. Nina, thank you for always being there for me, even when I had nothing but the joy of barbecue in my heart. You always supported me and have always been by my side. We built this together, and no one will ever take that from us. Thank you for trusting and believing in me throughout the years. The love I see in your eyes is the fuel that pushes me to succeed.

To my parents, Ron and Enola Horn, thank you for allowing me to dream as a kid. The foundation and principles you instilled have continuously guided me to this day. To my brother and sister, I love you both. Thank you, Cambrea, for always being there for me. All the sacrifices you made are a testament to the wonderful person you are.

CONTENTS

3

SIDES

4

PICKLES TO SERVE WITH YOUR 'Q

5

DESSERTS

6

SAUCES AND RUBS

RIP to my dear friend Marvin Lau

ACKNOWLEDGMENTS

This book would not exist without the contributions of so many wonderful people. From chefs, cooks, and dishwashers, to loyal guests and followers of the brand, to my investors who witnessed an obsession for the craft of barbecue and helped bring my vision to life. *Horn Barbecue* wouldn't be here without all of you. I would like to thank my grandparents, Alice and Mose, for allowing me to use your backyard as a classroom to teach myself the craft of barbecue. Thank you Ale Industries, Hangar 1 Vodka, Harmonic Brewing, and all the other breweries throughout the Bay Area that allowed me and my humble team to come and pop up over the years: your support helped us develop tremendously during those earlier days. I would also like to thank John and Sherri Kennedy, as well as Scott Schneider, for always being there to offer wisdom and support along this journey; you are loved. To the Maidenberg family, thank you sincerely for your support. To my photographer and friend Steven Pham, thank you for capturing my journey and being a pivotal part of my story. Andrew Thomas Lee, you are amazing my friend. Tan, thank you for everything. To my staff and anyone who has ever worked with me, I thank you all. Thank you Adrian Miller for your contributions to the culture of barbecue and for the amazing foreword.

A sincerest thank you to every chef and pitmaster who has inspired me on my journey and continues to do so today, including Rodney Scott, Helen Turner, Henry Perry, Aaron Franklin, Wayne Mueller, Esaul Ramos, Mark Black, Evan LeRoy, Tony Brown, Ed Mitchell, Ronnie Killen, Leonard Botello, Zach Hunter, Katie Button, Deborah and Mary Jones, Gordon Ramsay, David Chang, Carla Hall, Leah Chase, Pierre Thiam, Chris Shepherd, René Redzepi, Thomas Keller, Kevin Bludso, Elliott Moss, Andrew and Michelle Munoz, James Syhabout, Burt Bakman, Adam Perry Lang, Fermín Núñez, Geoffrey Lee, Pat Martin, Billy Durney, Nobu Matsuhisa, Daniel Boulud, Roy Choi, and Dominique Crenn.

FOREWORD

Matt Horn. I first came across his name in 2018 while working on a book about African American barbecue culture. I arduously searched for examples of Black men and women who were celebrated for their contributions to the time-honored tradition of cooking meats slowly over a smoky wood-fueled fire. Why? For decades, as barbecue experienced a meteoric rise in popularity, African Americans were minimized in, or left completely out of, the mounting number of print articles and television shows on the subject. Sadly, African American barbecuers weren't getting much love in the media.

Matt Horn was one of the few exceptions from the constant celebration of "White Guys Who Barbecue." I read the glowing online articles, and I was really impressed with his social media—the content, the beautiful photographs, and the level of engagement. I knew this brother was someone I needed to meet and interview and someone whose food I needed to taste. I reached out to Matt via social media, and I didn't expect to hear back for some time. Dudes on the rise are usually really busy. I was thrilled when Matt wrote back and, astonishingly, told me that he knew of me. Whuh??? Anyway, we had a great and encouraging back-and-forth and shared our mutual appreciation for each other. I made plans to visit the Bay Area and find out all that I could about the "West Coast Barbecue" that generated long lines at Horn Barbecue in Oakland, California.

That trip never happened. The COVID-19 pandemic upended everything, and the deadline to turn in the manuscript for my book *Black Smoke* passed before I could resume travel and gather with others. I was so disappointed that, in the last chapter of my book, I lamented the missed opportunity to write about what I fully expected to be a "next-level" experience. Matt seemed like a great example of someone who was rooted in tradition and looking toward the future, and I regretted not being able to interview him for that book.

Fast-forward to June 2021. The prestigious Commonwealth Club of California invited me to do a book talk in San Francisco. It was the club's first event since the pandemic began, and the event sold out within hours. As much as I'd like to take credit for the enthusiastic response, I'm pretty sure that having Matt and Nina, his wife, cater the event was a major factor. Regardless, I thought to myself, "FINALLY . . . I'll get to taste his food!" He didn't disappoint. On a blustery day, as the sun receded behind the San Francisco skyline, I joined a salivating crowd in grubbing on sliced beef brisket, pulled pork, coleslaw, collard greens, macaroni and cheese, and the surprise hit of the evening—smoked cauliflower. For a sweet finish, the Horns served up some pillowy banana pudding.

Just when I thought this dream couldn't get any better, Matt took me aside, told me that he was writing a cookbook, and asked for a favor. "Would you mind writing the foreword?" I gave him the "Brother Hug" (those who know, know) and answered with an enthusiastic "Yes!" I relished the opportunity to be part of such an important book. Remarkably, *Horn Barbecue* is only one of a handful of African American-authored barbecue books published in the last thirty years. Let that sink in for a moment, given the mountain of barbecue books published during that same time period. *Horn Barbecue* also inspires. In these pages, you'll read the story of a guy who had a dream, applied himself, and in a relatively short time, became very adept at a culinary craft that he loves.

Some of you are already familiar with the wondrous works of Matt Horn while others are being introduced to him for the first time. These days, people get called an "artisan" or a "pitmaster" when they really don't know what they're doing. Matt Horn is not one of those people. After you read this beautifully photographed and accessible book, you'll see why Matt is a rising star in the society of culinary artists who sublimely smoke meat. I'm tempted to write that he's "at the top of his craft," but that implies a finality that's misplaced in this context. Matt is more than ready to build on what the elders before him created and take barbecue in new directions. Are you ready for this soul-satisfying journey? I am!

—**Adrian Miller**
Author of *Soul Food: The Surprising Story of an American Cuisine, One Plate at a Time* and *Black Smoke: African Americans and the United States of Barbecue* and winner of a James Beard Book Award

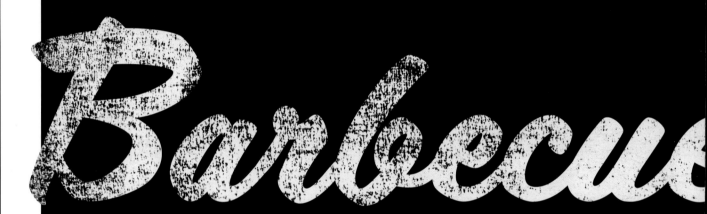

Barbecue

Introduction

MY BARBECUE JOURNEY

WHAT IS LIFE IF THE LIFE YOU ARE LIVING IS UNFULFILLING?

Ever since I was a kid, I have always tried to find purpose in every little thing that I do, whether it was building a fort or playing a simple game of basketball. "Am I doing what I am supposed to be doing?" I would ask myself. I asked the same question when I got older and was working at various retail jobs. I never felt that I was better than my coworkers, but I did feel my time and commitment would be better suited somewhere else. Eventually, when I discovered that I could work at making barbecue, I finally found a place where I could say, "Yes. I am doing what I am supposed to be doing."

But the journey to barbecue was a long one. I remember the exact moment I made the important decision to change my life. I wasn't being impulsive; the idea had consumed my mind for some time: I was going to quit my job. That beautiful fall Saturday in Los Angeles, about 8:00 p.m., was somehow the right time—after working all day. As my shift neared its end, I approached my last customer and, like hundreds before, walked them through selecting the perfect pair of shoes. My coworkers continued their tasks—oblivious to the fact that their manager was about to resign—and I knew they would be confused yet understanding. As we finished our closing duties, I left my keys, lanyard, and name badge neatly on the back desk, and with mixed emotions, I made my way out of the store for the last time. As I walked to my vehicle, I turned and looked back. This career had sustained me through the years but had never provided the fulfillment my soul yearned for. I needed to follow the truth in my heart, and at that moment, I didn't know whether I would succeed, but I was willing to take the leap.

I lived in Los Angeles at the time when food truck culture was exploding—and this exciting, boundary-busting cuisine, from Chef Roy Choi to the NoMad food truck, consumed me. I was an entrepreneur and dreamer, and I knew I wanted to start my own food truck business. Uninitiated into this world, I obviously needed advice, though, so I reached out to my uncle, a veteran in the restaurant industry. He quickly homed in on a crucial yet practical element of my dream with one pointed question: "What are you going to cook on this truck?" I realized in my excitement about the possibility of owning a truck, I had overlooked one glaring detail—the food.

After that call, I sat in my Inglewood, California, apartment contemplating what the best food to cook would be. At that point, I had cooked only burgers, breakfast, and spaghetti, which didn't really leave me inspired. Then, I asked myself this life-changing question: *Okay, Matt, if you could eat something every day, what would it be?* It took only a second to respond, without hesitation, out loud, in my quiet apartment, "If I could eat something every day . . . it would be *barbecue*." With those words, I got chills all over my body. *What was that feeling,* I wondered. That was my ah-ha moment, or it could have been the gentle breeze from the open window; either way, I was going to pursue the business of barbecue. But where would I start?

After a party to celebrate a boxing match, I invited a woman—Nina—whom I had met recently, to my place for a nice lunch. I decided to serve barbecue ribs, beans, and potato salad—anyone who knows me knows one of my favorite side dishes is potato salad. This was an ambitious menu because I didn't have anything to cook the ribs on. I knew my neighbor had a 20-inch (51 cm) Weber grill on the roof next to their satellite dish, so I asked to borrow it.

Lighter fluid, check; Kingsford charcoal, check; matches, check. I had watched both my grandfather and my father start fires and barbecue before, so how hard could it be?

I seasoned my St. Louis–cut ribs and then got the fire rolling. I arranged the meat on the grill, directly over the bed of hot coals and walked away. I had things to do to make everything perfect for my special guest. Once she was settled, I told her I was barbecuing and would be right back. I ran back to the roof and found ribs charred on one side from my lack of attention. I flipped the ribs, only to find the other side equally charred, so I pulled the slab off the grill and hustled back downstairs.

I had no idea what the hell to do with those ribs, so I covered them entirely with a bottle of barbecue sauce and cut them into pieces. Once the plates were ready, I handed Nina hers and dug into my own like a wild animal. When I finally looked up, it was clear she had only taken a small bite out of the ribs. Were they not good? Curious, I stopped eating and asked Nina how she liked the food. Nina's response was less than enthusiastic: "It's cool, thanks." When I asked why she wasn't eating the barbecue, she asked, "Do you want me to be honest with you?"

"Of course, be honest with me."

"The ribs aren't good." *Wow, did she just really say that*?

"What's wrong with them . . . exactly?"

"They are really tough."

How could I have ruined these ribs? I asked myself, *What could I have done better?* Questions flooded my mind; I couldn't think of anything else I could have done differently and had no answers. One thing I did know was I would

> "My barbecue journey began in my grandma's backyard and was driven forward by my own desire to teach myself how to make the best barbecue."

never let this happen again. If I wanted to be a great barbecue cook, I needed to train my mind and develop the skills necessary to be taken seriously. I committed myself instantly to the daily work and sacrifice required to take things to the next level and knew I couldn't achieve that living under my landlord's rules and constraints. So, I packed up and headed to the one place I knew I would be able to cook the barbecue I envisioned, 3½ hours north, to my grandmother's house in my hometown of Fresno, California.

AT MY GRANDMOTHER'S

When I was younger, my father's family held gatherings regularly, and whether a birthday, wedding, or funeral, barbecue and fried catfish were always on the menu. These gatherings often took place in my grandparents' backyard, so I knew many old pits were lying around just waiting to be fired up. When I arrived in my hometown, I headed first to Choices, one of my favorite markets, to grab some chicken, links, and ribs. I always imagined that the best food was prepared by making everything, such as rubs, sauces, and sides, from scratch. I was raised never to cut corners, and I wasn't about to begin today.

I remember being very excited about cooking and the opportunity to begin to learn about and explore barbecue and develop my own flavors and style. Upon entering my grandparents' backyard, I saw I was right—pits were everywhere. A small 24-inch (61 cm) rusted-out cooker that my father used to cook hot links and chicken caught my eye. I rolled it over to my cooking spot and lit the fire in the main chamber.

Like my rooftop ribs fiasco, I grilled the meat directly over hot coals and fire. I tried this technique several times and was frustrated that the desired result didn't match what I took off the grill. Rather than continue to ruin the meat, I sat by the cooker and wrote notes on precisely what I was doing to avoid the same mistake in the future.

My grandmother came out and asked how everything was going. I told her, "Great, Granny, just getting after it." She smiled and asked if I had tried the box attached to the cooker and explained my grandfather lit fires in that box, so it may be worth trying. She gestured to a nearby shed and told me my grandfather stored wood for the box in there. I had only been using charcoal, so the idea of using wood was an exciting new discovery. To my surprise, when I opened the shed, I found a cord of seasoned mesquite wood.

I didn't know anything about mesquite wood then. In my mind, it was a discovery, something to elevate my barbecue to the next level. So, I lit the fire, the same as I did every other time, but used this wood instead of charcoal. The mesquite was dry as a bone, so it ignited immediately. I noticed right away this fire had a different consumption than the charcoal. I put the meat over it, and I began to cook. I never got the results before that I got that day; there was something distinctive about the finished barbecue—the texture, the color, and the flavor were all exceptional. The incredible smell of the mesquite fire infused the meat. That weekend—days and nights—spent next to the smoke and fire, with B.B. King's music to keep me company, I became convinced that *this* was what I was supposed to do. Even without my grandmother popping out of the house every once in a while to exclaim that something smelled good, I knew I was on the right track.

I continued to cook in my grandmother's backyard for months, using the space as a school to teach myself. I learned the art of solitude, being one with the smoke and fire. When you are on these cooks, you have to find a way to pass the time. My cooks would often go all night, and in that time cooking, it allowed me to reflect on all facets of the cook.

I kept doing the same thing using wood, manipulating the air flow, damper on the stack, as well as the moisture within the cooking chamber. These things were constantly changing. They had to: No day was ever the same— some days it would be a sunny 75°F (24°C) or a windy 65°F (18°C). You have to trust your cooker to do its job while also exercising a measure of instinct during the cook. Your instinct will be developed the more cooks you have. You have to commit fully to learning and understanding the variables of cooking barbecue. Society has the impression that anyone can pick up a bag of charcoal, light a fire, throw the meat on, and then they are barbecuing. Although that may be true in some respects, there are very few people in this life who treat barbecue as a spiritual experience, like a beautiful journey through smoke.

During this time, it was essential for me to create and develop a personal flavor profile that

> **"I needed to make this work not only for myself but for my family."**

expressed the roots of my people: the smoking style of central Texas, heavily influenced by the flavors and dishes of the South. I called it "West Coast Barbecue." I never wanted to emulate or copy anything else or anything someone else was doing. I don't know why it was so important to me, but I've always done things my way—never cutting corners. I knew that to be truly great, there needed to be a measure of sacrifice. So, I committed myself to learning and refining as my way of sacrificing, giving up time spent with friends and family to focus on my newfound passion.

TO THE BAY AREA
My life was barbecue, and I was okay with that reality. But when my wife became pregnant with our first child, we knew driving back and forth to Fresno wasn't viable anymore, so we decided to move from Los Angeles. I became a father—another pivotal time in my life; holding my son and looking into his eyes made me realize my life didn't matter as much anymore. It was all about being the best that I could be for him and setting a positive example. I needed to be the best at what I did for him.

At that point, my wife's family— her mother and father—invited us to live in their home in Tracy, California. They wanted to help us get on our feet, as newlyweds and really young parents. I also looked at the move as the chance to have my own backyard to continue my barbecue obsession. It was a big decision because, being from Fresno in the Central Valley, I had never been to Tracy before; I didn't even know exactly where it was. But, we moved from Los Angeles to Tracy, arriving on a Wednesday with all our stuff. It was a change of scenery coming from Los Angeles, but we were excited about what was next for our young family.

On the Saturday after arriving in Tracy, my mother-in-law invited us to a farmers' market. It seemed like a good idea, but when I got there, my focus shifted from all the fruits and vegetables, and something I had been thinking about came forward. After all the time, sweat, frustration, and, finally, triumphs in my grandmother's backyard, I was ready to step out, to start selling my barbecue to the public. So, without telling my wife or anyone else, I signed us up to be a vendor at the farmers' market—the very next week! I had a small pit that I hired someone to fabricate, and in all honesty, it wasn't very efficient—but it was mine, and it would do. So, without much money to my name, I went online and ordered a tent, a cheap

cooler, and a couple of tables. All I needed now was to cook my signature barbecue and serve it.

We set up our black tent and proudly put up a sign that read "Horn BBQ." We had chicken pies, pulled pork sandwiches, spareribs, pit beans, potato salad, and slaw. We didn't sell a lot; maybe twelve people came by. But that was a huge moment for me, a step in the direction I knew I needed to go. It was very emotional. We kept coming back—for eight months—and the lines grew from tens to hundreds, people driving from all over making a day of it. That was the start.

I was learning a lot.

Love and patience are the two main ingredients for cooking amazing barbecue as well as living life. It is easy to want to rush the process and move on to the next thing. Barbecue isn't that for me—I submerged myself into the smoke and fire. There would be times I would be sitting on a stool in front of the firebox, eyes closed. I wasn't asleep; I was simply visualizing the cooking process and the result. I would envision my guests consuming the smoked meats and how their taste buds would respond. I cared about all those little details, and that is something that will separate you from a lot of the people that cook 'cue just because it seems like a cool thing to do.

HORN BARBECUE

24

The art, craft, and process of barbecue are an obsession to me. Every little detail is as important as the last. What do I want to accomplish with this cook. What do I want the finished product to taste like? These are the things that drive me during every cook. How does my smoke look? How is the bark forming during the cook? If you aren't intentional about what you want to accomplish in barbecue—or in life—you will live a life that is careless and unfulfilled.

When I made the decision to start doing pop-ups, we had already had a year under our belts doing farmers' markets along with a couple of festivals that did not work out terribly well—but which turned out to be learning experiences for me and my wife.

One of those festivals was a hog fest. I was extremely ambitious but very unprepared for the hog fest, but, what the hell, I decided, let's go for it. I didn't exactly know how much meat to prepare for this festival, so we tried our best to calculate the amount to cook. I bought eighty slabs of pork spareribs and thirty pork shoulders. I was so intent on making sure everything was fresh for our potential guests that I began cooking the morning of the event. I had never cooked that early before. I was confident that I had everything prepared and ready to go. I looked down at my watch and realized that the gates were opening. I looked at my wife and father, then said, "Let's do this." Only a few minutes

had passed when we started to see the festival fill up with people. Earlier that same year, when we would do the farmers' market, we were lucky to get five people in line at one—which was cause to celebrate back then—but here at the hog fest, I looked up and there were easily fifty people lined up at our 10' x 10' (3 x 3 m) food service tent with my little smoker next to it.

This was the moment I had been waiting for; we were knee-deep in the weeds, and, just as quickly as it began, it ended just as swiftly. *I was out of food and we had just gotten started. I can't believe this is happening to me right now.* My wife got on the phone and called her father and asked him to run to Costco to buy more meats. I don't know what was harder, running out two hours into the festival or having to tell the line of drunk and hungry guests that we had to shut down to prepare more food. Either way, it was definitely a learning experience that taught me how to improvise in a tough situation and also how to maintain composure in the midst of adversity.

We will always be faced with different circumstances in life. How we respond to those situations will determine the outcome. We could have panicked and quit, but we kept our composure and found a solution.

One thing I remember about the hog fest was a guest coming up to me and my father to compliment us on the food and offer some advice. I wasn't looking for any advice just then; we had to find a way to cook the next round of 'cue for the next guests who had decided they were willing to wait. He looked at me and said, "You know what you should do?" "What's that?" I asked. "Cook brisket," he replied. Oh, okay, brisket, yeah, for sure, I will look into it. *What's brisket?* I asked myself. I might have had brisket once in my life, over mashed potatoes and carrots. What I do recall is walking past these extremely large cuts of meat on my way to grab my spares and pork shoulders in Costco. But I was ready for a new challenge, so a few days after the festival ended, I went to Costco to find myself a brisket. The brisket was $57! I remember thinking that's a lot of money to do R&D on one cut of meat, but I bought it anyway. If I wanted to take my skills to the next level, I reasoned, I needed to accept challenges that were thrown at me.

The first brisket I ever cooked was untrimmed, and I cooked it too hot and too fast. I really didn't know what I was doing. But I kept trying and trying. The thing about a brisket that makes it so special is the patience you must bring to the long cooking process. There are so many things going on with a brisket while you are cooking it, and if any of the finer details are rushed, you will find yourself wasting time and money. The most important things that helped me develop my brisket were to stop worrying about the "stall" (see page 54), to stop overthinking the process, and to focus on what's important: cooking the meat. You want to watch the fire to make sure that you have oxygen-rich smoke flowing through your smoker. I always cook with a water pan; it helps add moisture into the cooking chamber throughout the long cooking process, and not just for briskets but also for spareribs and beef ribs. You don't want to lift the lid too much, which will cause fluctuations of temperature—consistency is key here. It's the little things that I focused on day in and day out. If you can learn to maintain consistency with anything you do in life, you have a skill that can easily be applied to the craft of barbecue.

"I'M QUITTING BARBECUE"

I can remember the really hot summer of 2016 in Tracy, the town in California where we live. At this point, we were done doing farmers' markets and we had a couple of music festivals under our belts. I decided I wanted to try doing pop-ups. I had been reading about restaurants doing pop-ups, and I felt like it would be an interesting concept for us. We started at Ralph's Bar in Tracy, off the main street right across from the high school. This busy, high-volume area seemed like a good place for us to set up and cook barbecue.

At that time, I was cooking spareribs, pulled pork, and brisket. When the date arrived for the first pop-up, I had been up all night cooking, and I was really excited to test out this new concept. It wasn't a comfortable place to start. The midsummer heat was intense. The 10' x 10' (3 x 3 m) black food tent was cramped. My wife was eight months pregnant at the time—but, as always, she was there by my side to help me set up and prepare. As time went by, the heat became unbearable, and I remember looking over at my wife and seeing sweat dripping from her forehead. It made me feel bad to have her out in this heat in the parking lot of a bar. I began to wonder if what I was trying to accomplish was realistic. I told her I thought it would be best if she just went home. Just before leaving, she asked me, "How much longer are you gonna be here?" I told her, "Until I sell out of this food." Prior to that day, I never had sold out, but I was determined to stay there and sell out of all the food.

It would've been really embarrassing to have had to take all the food back home. During that time, we were staying with my wife's parents, and I didn't want them to think that this thing, barbecue, that might have been perceived as a hobby was actually a waste of time if you tried to make a living at it. I don't know if it was pride or ego, but I ended up staying out there another three hours in the heat. During that time, I had a grand total of *one* customer who stopped and purchased some food. That covered my gas money for the day but nothing else. I realized I definitely wasn't going to sell out of this food today. I thought that maybe I shouldn't even be doing barbecue, and maybe I should start looking at doing something else in life.

As challenging as this period was—sleeping overnight at the farmers' market or the pop-up venue to watch the smoker, barely selling anything the next day—I still felt deeply committed to what I was doing. And there was also a pure joy and excitement in doing something new. I wasn't working a second job, and barbecue was the only thing that I was doing, so it made me feel bad at times to rely on my wife's full-time job. Yet I was committed to building something substantial, to making my barbecue into something great.

But I did think about quitting that day outside Ralph's. As I packed up all the hot food and the tent, I felt that I had completely wasted my time cooking overnight and then working all day in the tent. I asked myself again why I was even doing barbecue when I could be doing so many other things with my time. I needed to understand why I had chosen barbecue over other things.

The last thing I wanted to do was to go back home and have to explain to my wife's parents why I didn't sell all, or even much of, the food I'd bought and made. I was embarrassed. I felt humiliated. I felt like a disappointment. Yet, despite those feelings, I still felt that the only thing that gave me joy was the idea of serving people. In that spirit, I went to an area in the city where a lot of underserved people live, took out my table, and started yelling to anyone who could hear me, "Anybody hungry? Does anybody want any barbecue?"

And people came. In that moment, I realized that the true joy of barbecue consisted both of the journey of preparing the food but also the ability to feed someone—to be able to give something to someone and to be able to interact with that person. The thing about barbecue that will always consume me is the ability to be able to communicate with and get to know our customers. That connection with our customers continues to keep me going to this day.

DECIDING TO STICK IT OUT

That evening before I lay down for a bit, I decided that I was not going to do any more pop-ups. I was exhausted, and I felt defeated. I thought I needed an opportunity for me to stop everything that I was doing and reevaluate the direction I was going in my life. *I decided that I was going to finish what I started, simple as that.* It's what I was taught by my parents. My father would always tell me that you should finish what you start in life. And, to be honest, I didn't have the option or the luxury to quit. There was no plan B. This is what I decided to get into, and this is where I invested all of my time. I needed to make this work not only for myself but for my family.

I was exhausted—emotionally and physically—but driven by my sense of responsibility to honor those Black pitmasters who came before, carrying the torch, and continuing their rich tradition of barbecue. I am their story and want to represent the best.

That same night, after I finished feeding our second baby, I jumped on my laptop and began doing research. I found an article that talked about Black pitmasters being left out of the barbecue revolution that was happening in the United States. I read the article, and I was moved emotionally. How could the contributions of the many Black pitmasters who came before me be ignored? I mean, I grew up on barbecue: My father could barbecue, my uncles could barbecue, my grandparents cooked barbecue just as their parents and grandparents before them did. Barbecue has always brought us together whether in good times or bad. Barbecue always united my family, as it did many families across this country. How could the contributions of African Americans be ignored?

That article really resonated with me a short while thereafter when I came upon a list created by Fox News of the most influential pitmasters in the country. Not one was Black. Beginning in that moment, I felt I was in the right place. A light went off in my mind. I felt that I had found my purpose focusing solely on cooking barbecue and making *perfect* barbecue. After reading that article and others like it, I realized that what I was doing was much greater than myself. What I was doing was building on the legacy of the many Black men and women who came before me and worked the pits in the Deep South and all around this country. They provided me with an opportunity and a platform for me to move forward, to stand on their shoulders and create my own legacy. That's the reason why I am where I am today.

Without a purpose, without a substance to what you are looking for and trying to accomplish, life can be pretty meaningless. But now I know that barbecue was bigger than me—and that I wanted to leave my own impact on barbecue.

ESTD *Horn* 2015

BARBECUE

POP-UP

NOV
—
18TH

at ALE INDUSTRIES

IN OAKLAND

3 P M

'*til*
SOLD
OUT

SPACE IS LIMITED

TO MAKE A RESERVATION
DM @HORNBARBECUE
ON INSTAGRAM

DECIDING WHERE TO COOK NEXT

With this new realization and inspiration, I began reaching out to different venues throughout the San Francisco Bay Area. I knew that the Bay Area had a really great food scene. I felt like instead of remaining in the area of Tracy, on the outer fringes of the Bay Area, it would make sense for us to get closer to the heart of the area. Because barbecue and beer make such a great pairing, I prepared an email and, in one sitting, sent out thirty emails to different breweries. Unfortunately, I did not get any response that first evening, and I closed down my laptop for the night.

The next morning, I had one reply. It was from a brewery in Oakland called Ale Industries, and it said, "Hey, Matt, hope you're doing well. We would love to have you come out and do a pop-up at our brewery." I had never done much of anything in Oakland, but I thought that it made sense and that it would be the right market for my type of product. So we scheduled the pop-up, and I began preparing everything. This time it would be different: My wife wouldn't have to work the front of a tent, and I would not be in the back cooking. I decided I would cook everything and have it ready in advance so that I could then set up a butcher block and cut some 'cue personally for every guest with my wife as the cashier. I spent all night cooking all the different cuts of meat. At that time I was only using a 500-gallon offset smoker. I had brisket, spareribs, sausage, and pulled pork, along with two different sauces I made from scratch. Up to that day, and ever since, it has always been important for me to make everything from scratch. I never want to cut any corners or take a shortcut with our barbecue.

We didn't have a social media following at all at the time—maybe thirty followers at best, most of whom were friends and family. We made some flyers, and the brewery put the word out. We were expected to start selling at about noon. As we were setting up, I saw people lining up and I started to get a little nervous. This was the longest line we had ever had. I looked over to my wife and asked her, "Are we ready to go?" She smiled at me and shook her head yes. So I waved my right hand away to tell the first guest to come on up. "Hey, how you doing today? Welcome to our barbecue," I said. I was so nervous, but I was also filled with joy to see those people lined up. I got to work cutting the meats, trying to interact with our guests as I worked. There were lots of smiles, a lot of questions being asked, and even quite a few pictures being taken. It was cool. This was the moment I felt that I had stayed in the game for—the moment that made me feel like I was doing the right thing.

Something amazing happened that day. A really cool blogger came, and she told me this was some of the best barbecue this she had ever had—and she told me she was from Texas! That meant so much to me. But it also made me realize that there's always room to grow. The barbecue can always be better. That was and still is my way of disciplining myself and keeping my mind focused: I never, ever want to get complacent.

After she posted on her blog about our barbecue, things really began to take off. People were asking when and where the next pop-up was.

We were so excited. We just couldn't wait to do the next one! We did new pop-ups in other locations in Oakland and then in San Jose and San Francisco. Our online following started growing fast, and the crowds kept getting bigger. My only focus then—as now—has been to make sure that we deliver excellence to our guests day in and day out. There have been times I've been criticized for our long lines, but we stand by our process and will not cut corners. As long as you focus on excellence in anything you do in this life, everything else will follow. You're not always going to make everybody happy with what you do. But there will be people who do appreciate the work that you put in, your attention to detail, and the sacrifice and the time that it takes to create this product. There are people who are happy to see us every single day when we open up our doors, and that means everything.

WHAT I LEARNED FROM DOING POP-UPS

I won't pretend that the pop-up business is easy. In fact, it was always a challenge! But it was always just my wife and me and now and then some people we could find on Craigslist. Sometimes I would do an Instagram post and ask for volunteers. People would want to help out for a night or two, which was great, but we had no permanent help. For years, I had spent so many nights by myself working alone, like a farmer in his field, and tending my fire that it was hard to imagine myself in a different place with a full-time staff. It felt like a big risk, so I hesitated to rush into it. Put simply, the capital I always fell back on was my own time.

But I learned a lot from doing pop-ups. They taught me the importance of interacting with guests. I always loved doing that, and my background working in retail jobs helped. This interaction was the thing that drove our business forward—without our guests, we had no business. I always made sure that they felt welcome at our pop-ups, even as I worked hard concentrating on being the main cutter—and usually the only cutter. I try to give to my customers, and I find that they have a lot to give to me, too. Their stories of cooking and eating barbecue with parents and grandparents inspire me. Barbecue truly does connect people, and that is something that I have always appreciated about it.

Pop-ups taught us even more. I learned how to have the right equipment ready and how to keep it clean. I learned how to adjust to the big fluctuations in meat process and to make sure each day's budget worked. I learned that preparing early in the day for an efficient process later, when the guests arrived, was essential. In our pop-up days, I had only one cooker, which taught me lessons about how to pace the cooking over the course of the day and night— essential, because barbecue is, as you know, slow. (We still run into guests who think we start cooking a brisket at the moment they place their order!)

So, while there were many challenges to working in other people's spaces and not our own, doing pop-ups for so many years prepared us for the day that we would actually have a brick-and-mortar restaurant. I never wanted to have just any restaurant at all; I wanted only the restaurant that I dreamed of, a restaurant that would make me feel alive, and that is what I am fortunate to have now. My barbecue journey began in my grandma's backyard and was driven forward by my own desire to teach myself how to make the best barbecue, a kind of barbecue that was my own personal style and not someone else's, by help from my wife and our families, and, frankly, by my desperation and determination to get this thing right.

SMOKING
BASICS

TYPES OF SMOKERS

This section presents a quick overview of the types of smokers available. The best strategy I can offer when selecting a smoker is to do your research and look at models in person after defining your needs. Smokers can cost thousands of dollars, or you can spend a lot less and still stay within your budget by adapting your existing grill to smoke and consider upgrading your equipment after learning whether smoking is actually something you love. Start with an easy-to-handle smoker that allows you to cook at even, low temperatures and disperses the amount of smoke you need. Smokers to consider are:

Ceramic smoker: Also known as a Kamado grill or dome smoker, this versatile tool is a smoker, grill, and even an oven depending on the settings. These smokers use less fuel than others because they are compact in size, and their thick walls keep the heat inside. This smoker is less like a traditional smoker and more like a cooker that adapts to smoking.

Drum smoker: This tool is a charcoal smoker with a large fuel basket that holds enough fuel to burn all day. You add wood for the desired smoke. Beginners and experienced smoke enthusiasts can set up and use a drum smoker easily.

Electric smoker: This smoker can be pricey, but it allows you to control the temperature with just a touch of a dial, so less hands-on supervision while smoking is required. The smoke is produced by placing the wood in a chip tray, and the heating element in the unit does the rest. This smoker produces the least amount of smoke.

Offset smoker: You may have seen pitmasters in action using this classic charcoal briquette–fueled smoker if you watch barbecue cooking shows. They come in large and small versions and feature large chambers for the food with smaller fireboxes to one side—offset—for the smoke. You can drop several thousands of dollars on an offset smoker or get a more inexpensive version that requires more supervision. The benefit of this type of smoker is that you can add wood chips or chunks to the firebox without opening the lid of the compartment where the food sits. The heat can be uneven, slightly hotter closer to the firebox, and controlling airflow can take some practice, but the results are spectacular when you master this smoker.

Pellet smoker: This smoker option is expensive but has many features that make the added cost worth it if you want a more automated unit for smoking. Pellet smokers usually have digital controls for temperature control, meat probes, and alarms to indicate when the desired temperature is reached or cook time has ended. The fuel used with this smoker is compressed wood pellets loaded into a hopper that automatically feeds the fuel into the fire through an auger. You load it, set the time and temperature, and walk away. Pellet smokers produce abundant smoke and a constant, steady temperature.

Propane smoker: These smokers use a propane flame with an easy-to-use temperature dial to make pellets smolder and work like an electric smoker.

HOW TO TURN YOUR EXISTING GRILL INTO A SMOKER

You don't need a fancy, expensive smoker to create delicious meats. The bells and whistles on pellet smokers and other types of smokers take some of the guesswork out of the process, but they aren't necessary. Basically, to smoke, you need time and an indirect heat cooking method. You will probably need a temperature gauge to monitor the temperature inside the unit, and when buying meat, be aware that your space is limited—so don't get a massive brisket.

IF YOU HAVE A CHARCOAL GRILL . . .

Pile the charcoal on one side of the grill and place a drip pan on the other side. Light the charcoal and get the temperature of the grill to 250°F (120°C), no hotter. Fill the drip pan with ½ inch (1 cm) of liquid and place a layer of wood chips on the hot coals. Place your prepared meat over the drip pan and close the lid. If your grill has vents, keep them open; if it doesn't, leave a gap at the bottom of the lid for ventilation. Then, monitor the temperature in the grill, the temperature of the meat, and the smoke volume, adding charcoal and wood as needed.

IF YOU HAVE A GAS GRILL . . .

Preheat the grill with all the burners on for 10 to 15 minutes. Then, turn off the burners on one half of the grill and lower the burners on the other side until you create a grill temperature of 250°F (120°C). This might take some tweaking. Because you can't place wood chips directly onto the burners of a gas grill, put them in a metal pan and place the pan on the grill, above the lit burners. Also, place a pan filled with ½ inch (1 cm) of liquid in the middle of the grill. Place the prepared meat on the empty side of the grill and close the lid, allowing a gap for ventilation, or open the vents. Monitor the temperatures of the grill and meat as well as the smoke volume; adjust the heat with the burner dials and add more wood chips as needed.

BEST WOODS FOR SMOKING

Wood is one of the most critical components to smoking success; there are several factors to consider and no wrong choices, generally. I will not lay down strict wood rules because, depending on where you live, your choices may be limited. I often use a particular wood for a specific recipe, but that rule is not written in stone. You will start your fire with charcoal, usually lump charcoal, to get it going. But the added wood adds character and flavor to your meat.

WOOD VARIETIES
When choosing wood, the only hard-and-fast rule is to stick to hardwoods, generally deciduous trees that lose their leaves in the fall. Softwoods—evergreens—burn quickly and, due to their sap and higher moisture content, produce black acrid smoke, which is unsuitable in a smoker—and for food. If you have ever enjoyed a campfire with softwood, you will be familiar with the dramatic pops, spitting, and heaps of leftover ash; again, not ideal for smoking.

Hardwood is dense, dries well, smolders slowly, and releases clean and white smoke. The smoke also infuses food with the flavor you want. Different regions will have hardwoods native to that particular area, so you will be able to find at least one type to try in your smoker. You don't need to stick to one type of wood either; when you become more confident in the smoking process, get creative: Mix several varieties of wood to create complex flavors. The best hardwoods for smoking include:

- **Alder:** Found in the Pacific Northwest, this wood adds a sweet, light, delicate flavor to foods. It is particularly excellent for poultry, salmon, and trout.

- **Applewood:** This wood creates a mellow, mild, slightly sweet flavor. The smoke can take longer to permeate food, so watch it closely toward the end of the recommended cooking time. You don't want your food to jump from perfectly done to overly flavored. Try applewood with bacon, chicken, fish, ham, pork, and wildfowl.

- **Hickory:** Using this wood for smoking is common in the Midwest and in southern states because it is versatile and plentiful in these areas. It burns cleanly and is suitable for long cooks. Hickory smoke has a strong, sweetish flavor that can get unpleasantly bitter if you use too much of it. Be frugal when adding wood and ensure that there is plenty of ventilation. Hickory works well with ham, pork shoulders, poultry, red meat, ribs, and turkey.

- **Maple:** Maple is a mild wood that produces a subtle, sweetish smoke flavor. It will also add rich, burnished color to whatever you are smoking with it, which is very pleasing to the eye. The best food choices for smoking with maple are cheese, fish, game fowl, ham, pork, poultry, and vegetables.

- **Mesquite:** This wood is best used in smaller quantities or mixed with other woods. Mesquite produces lots of smoke and burns fast and hot. Mesquite smoke adds intense, earthy flavor, which can be overwhelming if you use too much. A good strategy for using mesquite for smoking is to add the wood closer to the end of a long cook or use it for quick cooks. Mesquite is popular for brisket (at the end of the cook), duck, game meat, lamb, steaks, and anything strongly flavored.

- **Oak:** Oak is often thought to be the gold standard of wood for smoking because it has a pleasing, distinct flavor but doesn't overpower the natural taste of the food. Oak is an excellent choice if you are new to smoking. The mellow flavor often takes a bit longer to emerge, so it is ideal for long cooks. Oak is suitable for almost any ingredient, including brisket, lamb, large beef cuts, pork, ribs, and sausages.

- **Other fruit woods:** Wood from fruit trees other than apple—cherry, peach, pear—burns faster and produces smoke that imparts a mild but distinctly fruity flavor that works best with products that do not have a naturally strong taste. So, this wood should probably not be your choice for brisket, although adding cherry as a supplemental wood creates a beautiful mahogany color to the meat. Try fruit woods with chicken, fish, pork, and turkey.

- **Pecan:** This wood imparts a strong flavor that is nutty, almost fruity, and sweet. It is often combined with other woods to tone down and balance its distinctive taste. Try pecan—mixed with other woods—for beef, chicken, fish, pork, ribs, and turkey.

WOOD SIZE

Choosing the wood size might be determined by your smoker—a pellet smoker, obviously, takes pellets—or availability or personal preference. The best choice is whatever hardwood is available in your region or sometimes in your own backyard if you cure it (dry it) correctly. Local barbecue suppliers, grocery or hardware stores, and online sources should be able to supply most of your wood needs. You have some choices when considering wood size, including:

- **Chips:** Like wood chunks, chips are used in conjunction with a bed of coals and are commonly used with electric smokers, gas grills, or propane. Chips burn fast, produce a lot of smoke, need to be replaced frequently, and add no heat. Chips are best for short smoking sessions.

- **Chunks:** Wood chunks are popular for smokers such as ceramic Kamado cookers, drums, and small offset smokers combined with a nice, hot bed of charcoal coals. Chunks are placed on the coals and burn slowly to produce the desired smoke and a bit of heat. This size of wood is ideal for long cooks that last all day.

- **Logs:** This can be the most challenging material to get unless you live in an area where wood is a common fuel source for heating homes. Logs are the largest choice for a smoker, and they often will not fit in commercial smokers unless those smokers are offset smokers designed for this type of wood product. Depending on the type of wood, logs will burn upward of 1½ hours in a well-insulated smoker. If you are a newbie smoker, you will probably not use whole logs.

- **Pellets:** If you have a pellet smoker, this is the wood choice for you. Make sure you pick up pellets designed for smokers rather than heating pellets because they are very different products. Pellets are made from compacted sawdust and can be one wood source, contain several types of wood, and even have flavored oils in the blend. Read the label to make sure you get what you want for your smoker. Pellets can burn hot, but pellet smokers are specifically designed to control the heat and smoke from their fuel, making them a good choice for beginners.

OTHER TOOLS NEEDED FOR BARBECUE

You have your smoker, fuel, and meat and are ready to get started. You might want to gather a few other culinary tools to make smoking easier and safer.

BRISTLE-FREE GRILL BRUSH
Cleaning your grill should be second nature after a cook, and this tool ensures you avoid small wire bristles in your food.

DUAL-PROBE THERMOMETER
A quality thermometer will simultaneously measure the temperature of the meat and the smoker. Get a wireless thermometer, if it is in your budget.

HEAT-RESISTANT GLOVES
These insulate your hands from heat and let you turn the meat without piercing it. You can also use thicker oven mitt–style gloves, but those don't have as much mobility.

INSTANT-READ THERMOMETER
You can place this tool in several spots to get an accurate read on temperature immediately. It is a must-have tool for grilling.

LARGE CUTTING BOARD OR BUTCHER'S BLOCK
Think about the size of a brisket and whether it will fit on a standard home cutting board. The answer is no. Look for a board with built-in grooves that catch the juices of whatever you are cutting.

MOP BRUSH
This is different from a pastry brush—the material is designed not to burn. Look for a brush with a longer handle and a removable absorbent head for both thin and thick sauces.

RIB RACKS
This might not seem like an essential tool, but smokers often do not have the space to hold more than a couple of racks of ribs. You can stand four rib racks upright on this device and still have excellent airflow while cooking.

SHARP, QUALITY KNIVES
You will be trimming and slicing meat a lot. A sharp knife is safer than a dull one. Look for knives with good weight and a comfortable handle for your hand. They are worth the investment.

TONGS
Get two or three sets of tongs, if possible, for food and charcoal. Pick up long, sturdy tongs—at least 16 inches (40 cm) long—so your hands aren't too close to the heat.

BEST TYPES AND CUTS OF MEAT FOR SMOKING

Smoking is a slow and low cooking process that takes tougher, fattier cuts of meat and turns them into succulent, delicious meals. You don't need to break the bank buying expensive grass-fed cuts to create a smoking masterpiece. Look for tons of fat marbling—intramuscular, not a fat cap—and collagen to tenderize and moisten the meat while it cooks. Cuts with large fat caps will not form the desirable crust, called "bark," on the outside of the meat, so you will have to trim off the cap (see page 50). When purchasing these tougher cuts, choose quality meat from a reputable source. Shy away from meats with fillers or preservatives, and make sure your poultry is not injected with a saline solution—this will ooze out of the bird as it smokes, creating an unpleasant taste. Some of the best meat choices for your smoker follow.

BEEF

Smoked beef is what people define as American barbecue; who hasn't seen mouthwatering slabs of beef—usually brisket—featured on cooking shows and in movies? It usually inspires you to want to run out and try it yourself! Beef is available in a vast range of cuts, textures, fat marbling, and flavors because its source is a huge animal. Each section of the animal, from cheeks to ribs to steaks, has its own character, and all options are spectacular when smoked.

- **Beef ribs:** Ribs are an excellent choice for beginners because they smoke quickly, and the meat is flavor-packed and tender with generous fat marbling. Because beef ribs have large bones, the heat is distributed evenly, creating a balanced cook. Look for chuck ribs, if possible, and cook them for 5 to 6 hours to an internal temperature of 205°F (96°C).

- **Brisket:** This is the ultimate cut for serious smoke enthusiasts, but it can be pricey, so don't try it until you are comfortable with smoking. Brisket is tough and fibrous, with extensive fat marbling that melts into the meat, creating succulent texture and incredible flavor. Brisket needs 10 to 12 hours in low heat, cooked to an internal temperature of 205°F (96°C) to produce the desired results, including that much-desired smoky crust.

- **Chuck:** This beef cut is from the shoulder and neck region, hardworking muscles that are incredibly tough unless cooked gently and slowly. Chuck is perfect for smoking, flavorful, and cheaper than brisket. Chuck roast is easier to cook because it is a smaller cut and can be served sliced or shredded after cooking for 5 to 6 hours. One of the best strategies when smoking chuck is to cook it to an internal temperature of 180°F (82°C) and let the carryover heat take it to 205°F (96°C) while it rests.

- **Flank steak:** This is a versatile, inexpensive cut with a strong beef flavor that holds up well to any smoke, even mesquite and hickory. Flank steak is best marinated for several hours before smoking it for about 3 hours to an internal temperature of 145°F (63°C).

- **Ox or beef cheeks:** It is worth the effort to find this ingredient because the tough connective tissue in the cut smokes to a tender texture, ideal for shredding into wraps and tacos. One method for cooking this cut is to smoke the cheeks for 3 hours to infuse them with flavor and then braise them for another 2 hours or so until they meltingly fall apart.

- **Top round:** This meat needs to be marinated or dry brined overnight before smoking because it is very tough and can dry out. Smoke this steak for 5 to 6 hours to an internal temperature of 150°F (65.5°C), let it rest for a minimum of 10 minutes, and then slice it against the grain.

- **Top sirloin steak:** Smoking steak? Certainly! This cut is less tender than more expensive steaks and can be smoked efficiently for about 1 hour per pound (454 g). Apply a rub to the meat and let it marinate for up to 24 hours in a sealed plastic bag in the refrigerator to add lots of flavor. Smoke the steak to an internal temperature of 145°F (63°C) and slice it thinly against the grain.

- **Tri-tip:** Tri-tip is a lean, chewy cut that requires a bit more work than other steaks for best results. This steak has so little fat, it does not caramelize like other cuts, so an extra step of searing is needed. For best results, season the meat well, smoke it for 2 hours to an internal temperature of 135°F (57°C), and then sear it well in a skillet with melted butter or on a grill to create a tasty crust.

FISH

Fatty fish from cold lakes and oceans are best for smoking because the fat layer keeps them moist while cooking and absorbs the delicious smoky taste. Fish can be brined and lightly seasoned before going into the smoker to enhance their flavor. The best choices for smoking are carp, mackerel, mullet, sablefish, salmon, sea bass, swordfish, trout, and tuna.

GAME AND EXOTIC MEATS

Almost anything can benefit from a bit of time in your smoker. Wild game meats have an assertive flavor, so they can handle most types of wood smoke. Some game meats can be leaner than commercially raised meats, so you can lard them with a little fat to achieve a tender, succulent result. Try draping venison in bacon, and make sure you wrap the meat in paper when it reaches 140°F to 145°F (60°C to 63°C) to keep the meat moist. Try bison, boar, duck, elk, rabbit, wildfowl, and even gator or ostrich in your smoker.

LAMB

Lamb is a fatty meat that lends itself well to smoking. Depending on your area, it can be pricey, especially in racks, which are perfect to wow guests or for a memorable meal.

- **Leg:** This cut generally weighs between 5 and 8 pounds (2 and 4 kg); it is thick on one end and thinner on the other, like you would expect from a leg. This size disparity can make it challenging to cook the leg evenly, though. Lamb is very fatty, has a strong flavor, and requires slightly less smoke because it can absorb too much. Brush the lamb with a mustard and herb glaze and smoke it for 3 to 4 hours for medium (145°F, or 63°C). Let the leg rest for 20 minutes before slicing it.

- **Rack of lamb:** This cut is elegant, especially if the bones are frenched (stripped of meat). Racks smoke quickly, in about 2 hours, and if you want the meat to be pink, take the internal temperature to 135°F (57°C).

- **Shoulder:** This cut is like a pig shoulder in size and can be pulled to create tasty fillings for sandwiches. Rubs and marinades work well with lamb. Smoke for 8 to 10 hours to an internal temperature of 203°F (95°C) if you want to shred the meat.

PREPARING THE MEAT

You don't have to spend hours getting meat ready before smoking it, but some preparation can create a better cook. The amount of time spent will depend on the cut of meat and desired result.

TRIMMING

Some trimming is required for ribs and large cuts. If you flip over a rack of ribs, you might see a thin membrane covering the bone side, which is called the silver skin. You should remove this membrane because it gets leathery when smoked and stops the smoke and seasonings from penetrating the meat. Slide a sharp knife underneath the membrane, lift it (sometimes grabbing it with a paper towel helps), and peel away the silver skin in one sheet.

Brisket and pork butt sometimes have a fat cap, which you might want to remove. Contrary to popular belief, this fat does not "melt" into the meat, and unless you are cooking the meat over higher, direct heat, the fat cap is not needed for protection. Leaving the fat cap on impedes the formation of the delicious bark. Trim off the fat cap with a sharp knife, trying to get as much as possible without removing any meat. Discard the fat.

TRUSSING (TYING)

This preparation technique refers to constraining poultry and large cuts of meat; you've probably purchased whole birds from the store that have had all their limbs trussed up in a compact package. Trussing is a good strategy for irregular cuts and whole birds because it creates an even surface for cooking, producing a uniformly cooked result. You can buy roasts like pork butt, as well as birds, already tied, so leave the string on when you place the meat in the smoker.

PORK

Pork is ideal for smoking because of its mild taste (it can be infused with many flavors), excellent fat marbling, and connective tissues. Some pork cuts to try in your smoker are:

- **Boston butt:** Although the term "Boston butt" is often used interchangeably with pork shoulder, a butt is a different cut. Pork butt is popular in the southern United States to make pulled pork and can be combined with almost any marinade, rub, or sauce. This inexpensive cut usually weighs between 11 and 13 pounds (5 and 6 kg) and should be smoked for 15 to 20 hours, depending on its weight, to an internal temperature between 195°F and 203°F (90.5°C and 95°C).

- **Ham:** When you think of ham on your holiday table, this is it. You can smoke both cooked and raw hams, depending on your timing and what you want as the result. Cooked ham can be brushed with brown sugar or a maple glaze and smoked for 2 to 3 hours to elevate the flavor. A raw ham can be brined and smoked for 7 to 8 hours, depending on its weight, until it reaches an internal temperature of 165°F (74°C).

- **Picnic ham:** This cut is from the upper front leg—it isn't a traditional ham from the rear leg—that is well-marbled, so it's also a forgiving cut for novice smokers. This inexpensive cut weighs about 10 to 13 pounds (4.5 to 6 kg) and is great for pulled pork. Smoke it for 10 to 12 hours to an internal temperature of 203°F (95°C).

- **Pork shoulder:** The shoulder is a fatty cut often used for pulled pork; it is a perfect beginner roast because it rarely dries out, even when smoked for very long periods. Pork shoulder comes in chunks weighing between 5 and 8 pounds (2 and 4 kg) and is relatively inexpensive. Season pork shoulder well or marinate it before smoking for 8 to 10 hours to an internal temperature of 203°F (95°C).

- **Ribs:** You have a choice here among baby back ribs, St. Louis–style ribs, and spareribs—all are delicious. St. Louis–style refers to a specific trimming method that squares off the ribs and cuts off the tips, and they're fattier and meatier, and so much more flavorful. Baby back ribs, which come from the backbone, are leaner, smaller, and typically more tender than spareribs. Ribs have excellent fat, connective tissue, meat balance, and bones that conduct heat, so they don't need as long in a smoker as larger cuts of meat. Try them seasoned, dry-rubbed, generously sauced, or all three at once! Smoke your ribs for 4 to 7 hours until they reach an internal temperature of 190°F (88°C). You can finish them off with a couple minutes on a grill if you like a charred presentation.

POULTRY

Poultry flavor is less robust than red meat, so it requires a more delicate smoke and less time in the smoker. If smoking breasts and thighs, I recommend brining them first to keep these cuts moist. Spatchcocking—flattening the entire bird—is an excellent method of preparation for smoking because doing so decreases the cooking time needed, and the smoky flavor is absorbed more easily. When cooking skin-on poultry, you can increase the smoker's temperature to about 300°F (149°C) to render the fat and create a delectable crispy skin.

- **Chicken:** Do not use too much smoke with chicken; the smoke will completely overpower the bird's natural flavor and taste bitter. Every chicken part can be smoked—whole, breast, leg, thigh, drumstick, and wing—just make sure you take the internal temperature to 165°F (74°C) without going over it by too much. This means your chicken will be food-safe yet still juicy.

- **Turkey:** This bird is incredible when smoked if you take the time to brine it before smoking. You can smoke turkey whole or cut it into smaller parts to create moist, smoked meat. Don't try to smoke turkeys weighing more than 14 pounds (6.3 kg) because they stay too long in the temperature danger zone (see page 52) as the bird heats up to 165°F (74°C).

FOOD SAFETY WHEN SMOKING

I want to address food safety briefly because, when working with food, you need to take steps to ensure whatever you serve is safe and delicious. If you cook regularly, the term "danger zone" should be familiar. This is the temperature range, 40°F to 140°F (4.4°C to 60°C) where food-borne bacteria multiply, so food should never stay in this temperature range for longer than 4 hours. Here are some safety rules to keep in mind so your smoking experience is safe:

- Smoking occurs at very low temperatures, so anything you put in the smoker should be thawed entirely first so it doesn't stay in the temperature danger zone too long. Don't thaw meat or poultry at room temperature—use the refrigerator—and only refrigerate raw meat or poultry for up to 2 days. If you need to thaw food in a hurry, you can submerge an airtight package in cold water (and change the water every 30 minutes) or place the package under constantly running cold water.

- Marinate your food in the refrigerator in a covered container. If you plan to baste while smoking, reserve some of the marinade for that purpose before you add the meat; don't use the portion with raw poultry or meat in it. Discard the used marinade.

- Always follow the manufacturer's directions for cleaning and preheating your smoker. Set your smoker in a well-ventilated area away from overhanging structures, trees, and shrubbery. Use the recommended fuel and approved fire starters (never gasoline) and insert a drip pan to prevent flares from dripping fat.

- Monitor the inside temperature of the smoker—most have a built-in thermometer—and check your meats and poultry with instant-read thermometers to ensure food-safe temperatures. Wait until after the surface of the food is past 140°F (60°C) to use an insertable probe because then you won't transfer pathogens from the uncooked outside of the meat to the inside of the meat when testing.

- Always smoke your food to the minimum safe temperature:

  > *Beef, bison, lamb, pork, veal, and venison should be smoked to a minimum internal temperature of 145°F (63°C).*

  > *Ground meat (beef, lamb, pork) and fish should be smoked to a minimum internal temperature of 160°F (71°C).*

  > *Poultry (whole, pieces, and ground) should be smoked to a minimum internal temperature of 165°F (74°C).*

- Refrigerate food within 2 hours after smoking it. Place food into shallow containers and cut large roasts and birds into smaller pieces so they chill more quickly. Always cover everything and use it within 4 days. If you aren't going to consume the cooked meat and poultry at that time, freeze it.

WHAT IS THE "STALL"?

When I first started smoking, I was obsessed with the "stall." I think I ruined the experience for myself because of this unnecessary stress. When I learned to let the smoking process happen and not worry about it so much, my finished roasts seemed to turn out better. You need to learn to trust your instincts, too.

So, what is this dreaded stall? When you put a large cut of meat in the smoker—like a brisket or a pork butt—and the internal temperature hits between 150°F and 165°F (65.5°C and 74°), it stops rising, and it can actually fall. This "stall" in temperature can last for a while, sometimes as long as 7 hours, before it swings up again. The internal temperature stalls from moisture evaporating from the meat—from the outside to the inside. This evaporating moisture balances the low thermal energy of the smoker, and voilà!—the stall. When enough moisture evaporates, the internal temperature will rise quickly, sometimes as fast as 30°F (about 17°C) in a couple of hours. Because you can't stop this plateau from happening, here are five strategies to deal with it:

1. Go with it—start smoking earlier than you need your meat to be done, and don't stress (my method).
2. Use smaller cuts of meat or separate briskets into flats and points. This creates an excellent bark on the point, but you don't get the satisfaction of that large, perfectly smoked whole brisket.
3. Smoke at a higher temperature—between 300°F and 350°F (149°C and 177°C)—so evaporation happens more quickly.
4. Wrap the brisket tightly in aluminum foil (the Texas crutch) when it hits the stall, stopping the evaporation. This will also impede the formation of that incredible crust, so when you reach the target temperature, unwrap the meat and put it back in the smoker so the bark can form somewhat.
5. You can also wrap the meat in unwaxed butcher's paper so the smoke can still get through this semipermeable covering. You won't stop all of the evaporation, so the meat can still stall, but it will plateau for a shorter time.

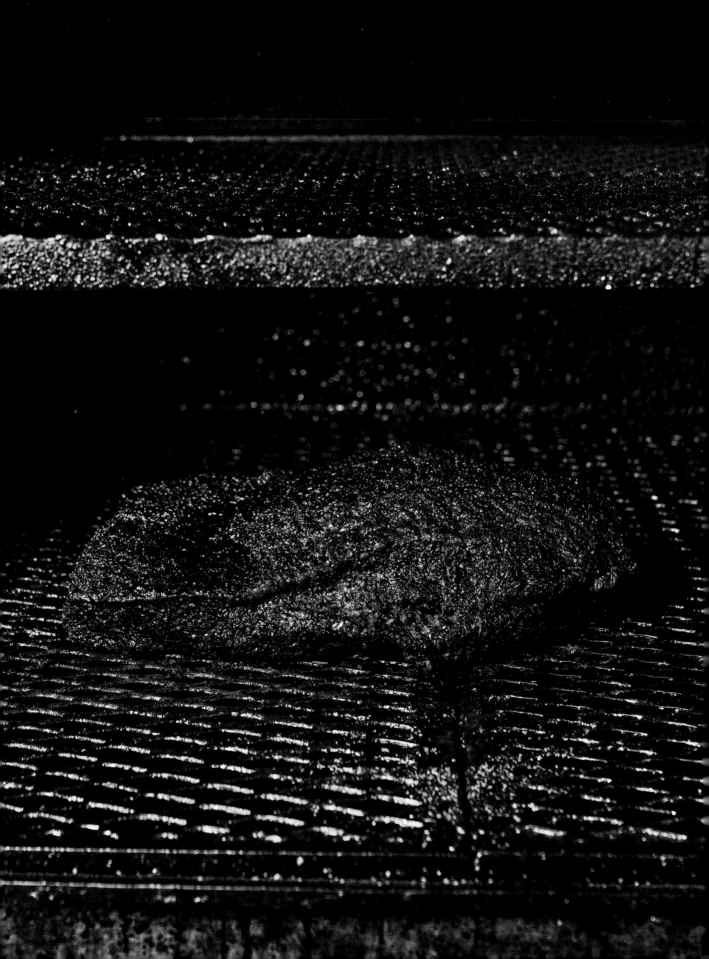

10 COMMON QUESTIONS ABOUT SMOKING

1. **What is the first step when I get a new smoker?**
Read the manual that came with your smoker, front to back. Then, clean all the surfaces and anything removable from the smoker, like the grates, lid, and sides. Season the grates with a thin layer of canola or avocado oil and wipe it off with a paper towel. Do a test burn without food; follow the directions provided by the manufacturer in the manual.

2. **Can I use bagged wood or green wood?**
Fresh-cut wood—green wood—usually has too much moisture to be effective; cured wood is recommended. Most bagged wood is kiln-dried, so it burns too quickly to be an effective smoking agent.

3. **Should I soak my chips or chunks?**
The short answer is no, but if a manufacturer recommends soaking, then soak. Water takes a very long time to penetrate wood—it only goes in about ⅛ inch (0.3 cm)—so soaking can be ineffective. Plus, the energy required to steam the water off the wood can alter the cooking temperature of your smoker.

4. **What's hot and cold smoking?**
Hot smoking is what most people imagine when smoking meat; it adds a smoky flavor and cooks the meat in a temperature range higher than a food-safe temperature of 200°F (93°C). Cold smoking only flavors the meat, or other foods like cheese, with a smoky character and is done at lower temperatures, increasing the chance of dangerous bacteria growth, such as botulism.

5. **Should I use a water/drip pan?**
Some smokers recommend water pans—and may include removable drip pans in the smoker—and using them is good practice, especially when smoking for an extended time. Large disposable aluminum foil roasting pans are excellent for this task and reduce cleanup. The liquid in the pan can stabilize the temperature in the smoker and add humidity. Stick to about ½ inch (1 cm) of liquid so the ambient temperature doesn't fall too much; more liquid equals lower temperatures, which means longer cook times. Plain water is standard, but you can mix it with apple cider vinegar, apple juice, herbs, or pineapple juice to add extra flavor to whatever you smoke.

6. **How much smoke is enough?**

   You want to control the smoke to produce the best results. Too much smoke can create acrid-tasting meat, so add a few wood chunks or chips at a time to the smoker. You also don't want thick, dark smoke; gently flowing white smoke is most desirable. The smoke should not be trapped; it should be able to move around and escape the smoker. Your smoker needs adequate ventilation, so experiment with the vents to create the correct ratio and good combustion. You can always close the vents if your fire gets too hot.

7. **Can I put cold meat in the smoker?**

   You can if you are smoking the meat all day, but it is not the best idea. Room-temperature meat becomes infused with the desired smoked flavor more easily, and the interior of the meat comes to a safe temperature (see page 52) more quickly. Never smoke meat or poultry from frozen.

8. **Should I check my meat?**

   Smoking is different from roasting or grilling, where the temperature is 400°F (204°C) or higher, and meat can burn; most smoking occurs at 200°F (93°C) or so, which is a gentle, low temperature. A lower temperature means you don't have to supervise or open the smoker multiple times. Opening the smoker lets out a great deal of heat, so cooking time is affected negatively. Many smokers have probes to insert into the meat—some allow you to set an alarm when the meat reaches the desired internal temperature—and most smokers have gauges on the outside that indicate the interior temperature of the smoker.

9. **Should I wrap my brisket?**

   I like to wrap my brisket about two-thirds of the way through smoking (see page 91) to avoid losing moisture, but it is a personal preference. If you like an extra smoky, crispy exterior, skip this step. I usually use unwaxed butcher's paper to wrap the meat because it allows the meat space to breathe; aluminum foil creates too tight of a seal that can impede bark formation.

10. **What if I don't get the results I want?**

    Smoking meat takes practice and time and can be affected by many choices and factors. The recipes in this book should yield delicious results because I've tested and retested them. That said, your palate and taste might be different from mine, so feel free to make adjustments after sampling the original recipe. You might want to start a smoking journal or make notes on an app to document the results of the recipes you cook. This can include details such as the protein used, whether it was marinated (and in what) or unmarinated, type of wood used, wrapped or unwrapped, temperature, and time. Tweak, refine, enjoy the process, and most important, trust your instincts.

SEASONINGS, BRINES AND MARINADES, RUBS, MOPS, AND SAUCES

Everyone has a personal preference when it comes to what goes on their food before it goes into the smoke as well as after it emerges from the smoker. There is no right or wrong answer, but at a minimum, salt is a culinary essential.

Salt brings out flavor in food; it wakes up our taste buds and enhances the experience of eating. If you don't have a dietary condition that limits salt, season generously with it. If you aren't using any other flavorings, also add on a sprinkle of freshly ground black pepper.

Brines can be dry or wet and work well with low-fat foods such as fish and poultry.

Dry brining is applying salt to the food and letting the food sit so the salt can penetrate it. This process is called denaturation—when proteins are broken down—and it creates a juicy, rich result.

Wet brines and marinades are similar treatments, with the amount of salt being the real difference. Brines contain generous amounts of salt. Brines and marinades are a mixture of salt, water, and other aromatics, like spices and herbs. Acid, in the form of citrus juice, fruit juice, or vinegar, is often added as well. This mixture tenderizes the meat as it sits in the liquid. Don't leave fish in a brine or marinade for longer than 1 hour, or poultry for more than 12 hours, or you can get a mushy texture.

Dry rubs are a favorite treatment in my restaurant—we even have a special one you can purchase that we refined and tested until it was just right. Unlike salt, dry rubs stay on the surface of the meat, so you apply them just before smoking. You want a combination of ingredients that don't overpower whatever you are putting the rub on. Garlic, onion, paprika, pepper, salt, and sugar are a good start. Experiment with flavors you enjoy and create your own recipes, or pick up a store-bought favorite.

A mop (see page 215) is a basting sauce that adds flavor and keeps the meat moist. It is a thin sauce that doesn't obscure the seasonings like a thick barbecue sauce can. Mops are used with red meat and are applied every hour or so while smoking to help create that desirable crust. Some mop combinations include fruit juice, herbs, oil, spices, sugar, tomato, vinegar, or even cola or other soda to help with caramelization from the sugar.

Sauces are an important component of Horn BBQ, and this book has some of my favorites (see chapter 6). Many regional recipes do not include sauce—think parts of Texas—but sauce can add an extra flavor element and elevate the finished product. Don't sauce too soon, though; wait until 15 to 30 minutes before the meat is done. This creates a sticky sauce that adheres nicely to the meat but not a hard, overly smoky finish or burned sauce.

MY TOP TIPS FOR THE VERY BEST BARBECUE

My style of barbecue is a melding of Louisiana, Oklahoma, and Texas traditions, which all display their own characteristics and flavors. No matter the regional idiosyncrasies of barbecue, I've learned some essential tips that cross all types to ensure barbecue success in your backyard.

1. **Don't wash the meat.**
   Washing meat, in general, is not a food-safe practice; any water that splashes from the meat can be crammed with bacteria, cross-contaminating everything it lands on. So, don't do it. Washing meat also dilutes the meat's flavor because it waterlogs the protein. Use paper towels to pat any excess moisture off the meat, discard the towels, and wash your hands. Then, season the surface and you are good to go.

2. **Don't overseason the meat.**
   When you smoke meat, poultry, and fish, the goal is to achieve that signature smoky flavor and, of course, taste the natural flavor of the protein. Why compete with that by adding too much seasoning? My go-to seasoning is a salt and pepper base with granulated onion and garlic and perhaps a touch of sugar, depending on what I'm throwing in the smoker. The sugar enhances the Maillard reaction (a chemical reaction between the heated protein and carbohydrates) that creates color, browning—flavor—as the protein in the meat reacts to the sugar.

3. **Control the temperature.**
   Most meats smoke beautifully between 225°F and 245°F (107°C and 118°C), so keeping the smoker's temperature in that range is crucial. A remote thermometer can be a lifesaver—especially if you are a novice smoker—because you can adjust factors to ensure the meat turns out how you want it. If you need a higher temperature, you can vent some air by raising the lid slightly or opening the air vents (if this is a feature of your smoker). If you need to lower the temperature, close the vents or close the lid.

4. **Let the coals get hot.**
   Coals should burn until completely white to burn off the charcoal. Black coals will produce harsh-tasting meat rather than the smooth smoke flavor required for successful barbecue.

5. **Control the smoke.**
   All smoke is not created equally; you are looking for the pure-white smoke from those white coals and controlled temperature within the smoker. There should only be a small stream of white smoke coming out of the smoker, not billows. If there is too much smoke, reduce the temperature (see above). The meat will dry out with excessive smoke, and the flavor will be too strong, which is unpleasant. Too little smoke defeats the purpose because you won't get that signature smoky taste. Try replacing the wood in the smoker. It is either burned out, or there is not enough.

6. **Don't crowd the smoker or flip the meat too soon.**
   There needs to be airflow all around the protein for the Maillard reaction to occur. If your meat pieces are crammed together, this reaction will not happen. Meat needs its own access to the heat source. Leave the meat alone until it has a dark, charred outside crust; then, flip it. Patience is key.

7. **Don't keep opening the smoker.**
   Of course, you will need to add more wood, mop the meat, or fill the water pan while smoking, but do these tasks as quickly as possible. Each time the smoker is opened, you lose heat and the temperature drops. This increases the cooking time. Be efficient!

8. **Let the meat rest.**
   If you want juicy meat and poultry, you need to allow it a bit of time after cooking to reabsorb its juices. If you cut your barbecue immediately after cooking it, all you will get is a dry product and lots of delicious juice spilling onto the cutting board.

PART
TWO

THE

MEATS
AND
BIRDS

IN THIS CHAPTER,

you will find meat on the menu at my restaurant and some that are served for family events or as a quiet meal at home. Sausages bursting with juice, spices, and flavor; crackling, tender ribs; Southern favorites such as oxtails and smoked pig feet; and the deeply flavored, delectably crusted brisket that started my smoking obsession. Each of these dishes was created from hours of testing, tweaking, overcoming, and improving on less-than-perfect results. Maybe this is the start of your passion for barbecue—enjoy the journey.

You will need to invest in (or borrow) a meat grinder (I like LEM grinders for the integrity of their equipment and the ability to handle heavy use), sausage stuffer, and casings for this recipe and several others in the book, but making the investment is well worth it. I like to create a complex, rich flavor in my hot links with a combination of beef and pork. Experiment with one or the other to make your signature links. Serve your newly smoked links on a piece of white bread with some of your favorite barbecue sauce (or try one of my favorites; see chapter 6) spooned on top and with more on the side for dipping, if you like.

YIELD:
SERVES 6 TO 8

PREP TIME:
2 HOURS, PLUS 3 HOURS
TO CHILL

COOK TIME:
30 MINUTES TO 1 HOUR

HOT LINKS
FROM SCRATCH

1. Cut the pork and beef trimmings into ½-inch (1 cm) cubes. In a large bowl, combine the cubed meat, paprika, pepper, granulated garlic, salt, ground mustard, chili powder, and water and mix thoroughly. Cover the bowl and refrigerate for at least 3 hours, or overnight for the following day.
2. About 30 minutes before you're ready to stuff the sausage, rinse the casings, place them in a large bowl, and add enough warm water to cover. Let soak for 30 minutes to loosen. Drain.
3. Run the meat through a meat grinder on the coarse setting according to the manufacturer's instructions.
4. Using your hands, mix the ground meat thoroughly; it should stick together when pressed.
5. Feed the casings onto the stuffing tube, tying off the end of the casing before you begin. (I use a medium-size stuffer at the restaurant.) Poke a small hole near the tied end of the casing to prevent air buildup while stuffing. Stuff the casings, then pinch and twist the links, making the links about 6 inches (15 cm) long.
6. Preheat the smoker to 225°F (107°C).
7. Place the links in the smoker and smoke for 30 minutes to 1 hour until they reach an internal temperature of 165°F (74°C). They should be a beautiful red color.

1½ pounds (681 g) pork butt or shoulder

8 ounces (225 g) brisket trimmings

3 tablespoons (25 g) paprika

2 teaspoons coarse black pepper

2 teaspoons granulated garlic

2 teaspoons kosher salt

2 teaspoons ground mustard

2 teaspoons chili powder

⅓ cup (80 ml) water

All-natural hog casings, for stuffing

YIELD:
MAKES ABOUT 18 LINKS

PREP TIME:
2 HOURS

COOK TIME:
30 MINUTES TO 1 HOUR

This pork sausage is spicy with cooling chunks of cheddar; when you bite into a link, the cheese oozes out with the delicious juices. This recipe makes a heap of sausages—depending on your casing size—that can be frozen after smoking or before. If you want to make fewer links, cut the recipe in half.

JALAPEÑO CHEDDAR LINKS

5 pounds (2 kg) pork shoulder, cubed

Natural hog casings, for stuffing

5 tablespoons (30 g) coarse black pepper

3 tablespoons (54 g) kosher salt

3 tablespoons (21 g) onion powder

3 tablespoons (27 g) garlic powder

2 teaspoons cayenne pepper

2 teaspoons smoked paprika

1 cup (125 g) cubed smoked cheddar cheese

½ cup (45 g) chopped jalapeño pepper

¼ cup (25 g) chopped scallion, white and green parts

1. Place the pork in the freezer for 30 minutes to firm up before grinding.
2. About 30 minutes before you're ready to stuff the sausage, rinse the casings, place them in a large bowl, and add enough warm water to cover. Let soak for 30 minutes to loosen. Drain.
3. Grind the pork into a large bowl. (I like to use the coarse attachment on my grinder.) Add the black pepper, salt, onion powder, garlic powder, cayenne, and paprika. Using your hands, mix the pork to disperse the seasonings evenly throughout the meat.
4. Add the cheddar, jalapeño, and scallion and mix to incorporate.
5. Feed the casings onto the stuffing tube, tying off the end of the casing before you begin. (I use a medium-size stuffer at the restaurant.) Poke a small hole near the tied end of the casing to prevent air buildup while stuffing. Stuff the casings, then pinch and twist the links, creating about eighteen (6- to 8-inch, or 50 to 20 cm) links.
6. Refrigerate the links overnight in a sealed container, or smoke them at 250°F (121°C) for 30 minutes to 1 hour until they reach an internal temperature of 160°F (71°C). You can also grill the links over medium-high heat for about 20 minutes, turning several times while cooking, until they reach an internal temperature of 160°F (71°C).

From left: Hot Link, Jalapeño Cheddar Link, and Andouille Link

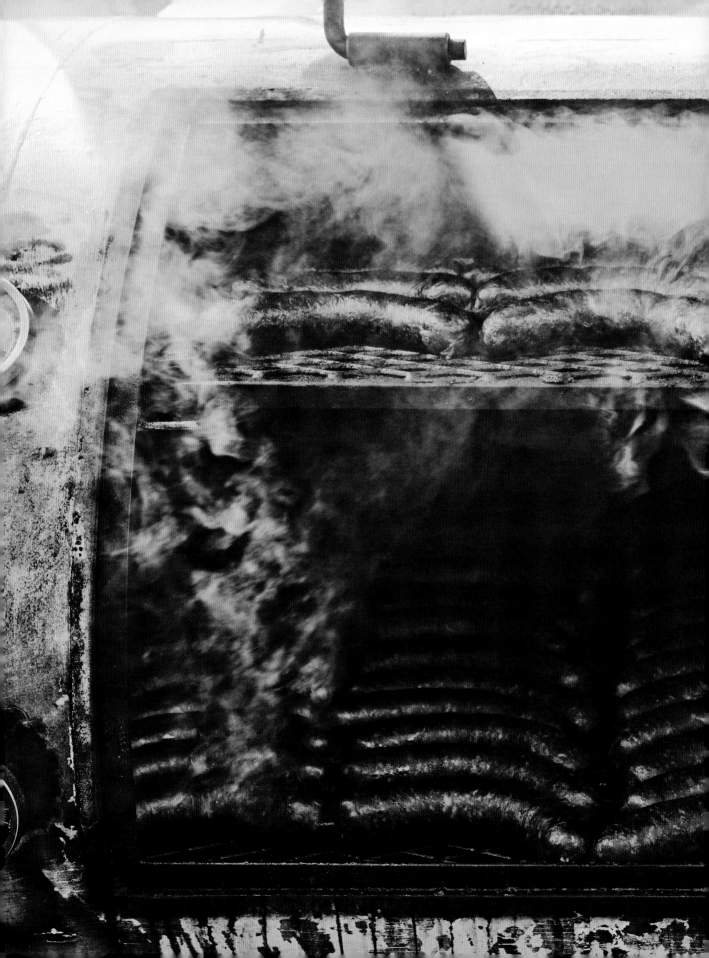

YIELD: MAKES ABOUT 24 LINKS

PREP TIME: 2 HOURS

COOK TIME: 30 MINUTES TO 1 HOUR

This sausage has its roots in France, so it should be no surprise that it turns up often in Louisiana Cajun cooking. The pork belly adds rich fat to the mixture and the milk powder acts as a binder, so don't omit it.

ANDOUILLE LINKS

5 pounds (2 kg) pork shoulder, cubed

Natural hog casings, for stuffing

2 pounds (908 g) pork belly

⅓ cup (40 g) milk powder

5 tablespoons (30 g) coarse black pepper

3 tablespoons (54 g) kosher salt

3 tablespoons (21 g) onion powder

3 tablespoons (30 g) minced garlic

3 tablespoons (27 g) ground mustard

2 tablespoons (11 g) cayenne pepper

1 tablespoon plus 2 teaspoons (14 g) sweet paprika

1. Place the pork shoulder cubes in the freezer for 30 minutes to firm up before grinding.
2. About 30 minutes before you're ready to stuff the sausage, rinse the casings, place them in a large bowl, and add enough warm water to cover. Let soak for 30 minutes to loosen. Drain.
3. Grind the pork cubes and pork belly into a large bowl. (I like to use the coarse attachment on my grinder.) Add the milk powder, black pepper, salt, onion powder, garlic, ground mustard, cayenne, and paprika. Using your hands, mix the pork to disperse the seasonings evenly throughout the meat.
4. Feed the casings onto the stuffing tube, tying off the end of the casing before you begin. (I use a medium-size stuffer at the restaurant.) Poke a small hole near the tied end of the casing to prevent air buildup while stuffing. Stuff the casings, then pinch and twist the links, creating about 24 (6- to 8-inch, or 15 to 20 cm) links.
5. Refrigerate the links overnight in a sealed container, or smoke them at 250°F (121°C) for 30 minutes to 1 hour until they reach an internal temperature of 160°F (71°C). You can also grill the links over medium-high heat for about 20 minutes, turning several times while cooking, until they reach an internal temperature of 160°F (71°C).

This is another Cajun creation. This sausage is packed with pork, chicken liver, vegetables, and a fair bit of cooked white rice. You will cook the meat and liver before tossing together the sausage mixture, a different process than the other links in this book. The best part of using cooked ingredients is you can taste the mixture before stuffing the casings and adjust the seasonings as needed.

YIELD: MAKES ABOUT 24 LINKS

PREP TIME: 3 HOURS

COOK TIME: 30 MINUTES TO 1 HOUR

BOUDIN LINKS

1. In a stockpot, combine the pork, celery, onion, bell pepper, garlic, salt, and enough water to cover by about 2 inches (5 cm). Bring to a boil over medium-high heat, turn the heat to low, and simmer for 1 hour.
2. Add the chicken liver and simmer for about 45 minutes until the pork is tender.
3. About 30 minutes before you're ready to stuff the sausage, rinse the casings, place them in a large bowl, and add enough warm water to cover. Let soak for 30 minutes to loosen. Drain.
4. Drain the meat and vegetables into a large bowl and reserve the liquid. Transfer the meat and vegetables to a cutting board, or food processor, and finely chop them. You can also run them through a meat grinder set for a coarse grind.
5. Transfer the chopped meat and vegetables to a large bowl and add 1 cup (240 ml) of the reserved cooking liquid, the cooked rice, black pepper, milk powder, cayenne, and paprika. Stir the ingredients to combine until the mixture is slightly sticky and moist. If it is too dry, add up to ½ cup (120 ml) more of the reserved liquid.
6. Feed the casings onto the stuffing tube, tying off the end of the casing before you begin. (I use a medium-size stuffer at the restaurant.) Poke a small hole near the tied end of the casing to prevent air buildup while stuffing. Stuff the casings, then pinch and twist the links, creating about 24 (6- to 8-inch, or 15 to 20 cm) links.
7. Refrigerate the links overnight in a sealed container, or smoke them at 250°F (121°C) for 30 minutes to 1 hour until they reach an internal temperature of 160°F (71°C). You can also grill the links over medium-high heat for about 20 minutes, turning several times while cooking, until they reach an internal temperature of 160°F (71°C).

5 pounds (2 g) pork shoulder, cubed

3 celery stalks

1 sweet onion, quartered

1 green bell pepper, halved and seeded

2 garlic cloves, peeled

3 tablespoons (54 g) kosher salt

2 pounds (908 g) chicken liver

Natural hog casings, for stuffing

2 cups (370 g) cooked white rice

5 tablespoons (30 g) coarse black pepper

¼ cup (30 g) milk powder

2 tablespoons (11 g) cayenne pepper

2 tablespoons (17 g) sweet paprika

Tri-tip steak was popularized more than seventy years ago in open Santa Maria–style pits; it is so often associated with this region of California that you can ask for it as a "Santa Maria cut" or "California cut." My strategy here is to treat the steak to my brisket technique and create a tender, smoked steak ideal for a family-style meal.

YIELD: SERVES 6

PREP TIME: 20 MINUTES

COOK TIME: 25 MINUTES, PLUS 20 MINUTES TO REST

SMOKED TRI-TIP

1. Preheat the smoker to 300°F (149°C). Make sure you are burning a clean oxygen-rich fire.
2. In a small bowl, stir together the salt, pepper, garlic powder, onion powder, and oregano until well blended.
3. Trim any loose fat from the tri-tip. Rub the meat with olive oil and evenly apply the rub on all sides.
4. Place the tri-tip in the smoker and smoke for 20 to 25 minutes until it reaches an internal temp of 135°F (57°), checking it periodically. Once done, remove the meat from the smoker, wrap it in aluminum foil, and let it rest for 20 minutes.
5. Unwrap the meat and slice it against the grain to serve.

2 tablespoons (36 g) coarse kosher salt

2 tablespoons (12 g) coarse black pepper

1 tablespoon (9 g) garlic powder

1 tablespoon (7 g) onion powder

1 tablespoon (3 g) dried oregano leaves

1 (3- to 5-pound, or 1 to 2 kg) tri-tip steak

Olive oil, for the steak

HOW TO
PREPARE PERFECTLY SMOKED SPARERIBS.
Full recipe follows on page 82.

1. Trimming the breastbone from the spareribs.
2. Pulling the skin off the back of the spareribs.
3. Trimming and shaping the spareribs.
4. Rubbing mustard bind onto the ribs.
5. Seasoned spareribs.
6. Saucing the ribs before the wrap.
7. Wrapping the ribs.
8. Saucing the spareribs midway through the cook.
9. Finished spareribs.

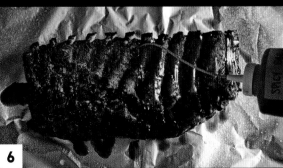

This recipe is easily scalable to include more than one rack of ribs, depending on how many people you want to feed or how hungry you are. Spareribs are an excellent meat to start with if you are unfamiliar with smoking; you do not have to commit an entire day to the process before enjoying that smoky, tender rack.

PERFECTLY SMOKED
SPARERIBS

2 tablespoons (36 g) coarse kosher salt

2 tablespoons (12 g) coarse black pepper

2 tablespoons (18 g) garlic powder

2 tablespoons (14 g) onion powder

2 tablespoons (17 g) paprika

2 tablespoons (18 g) ground mustard

1 tablespoon (7 g) ground cinnamon

1 (3- to 4-pound, or 1 to 2 kg) rack pork spareribs

Mustard or olive oil, for the ribs

Water, apple juice, or apple cider vinegar, for spritzing

1. Preheat the smoker to 275°F (135°C). Make sure you are burning a clean oxygen-rich fire.
2. In a small bowl, stir together the salt, pepper, garlic powder, onion powder, paprika, ground mustard, and cinnamon until well blended.
3. Trim any loose fat from the ribs. Remove the skirt meat from the back of the spareribs, or it can be left on—it's your choice.
4. Rub the ribs with mustard or olive oil and season the meat evenly all over with the rub.
5. Place the seasoned ribs in the smoker and don't open it for 4 hours. After 4 hours, spritz the ribs with water, apple juice, or vinegar. Check for color—the ribs should look like a beautiful mahogany color. Barbecue is more than food—it tells a story, transcends you, and is a work of art that can present beautiful colors and textures.
6. Cook the ribs until they reach an internal temperature of 200°F (93°C), then remove them from the smoker, wrap the rack in aluminum foil, and let them rest for 30 minutes.
7. Serve.

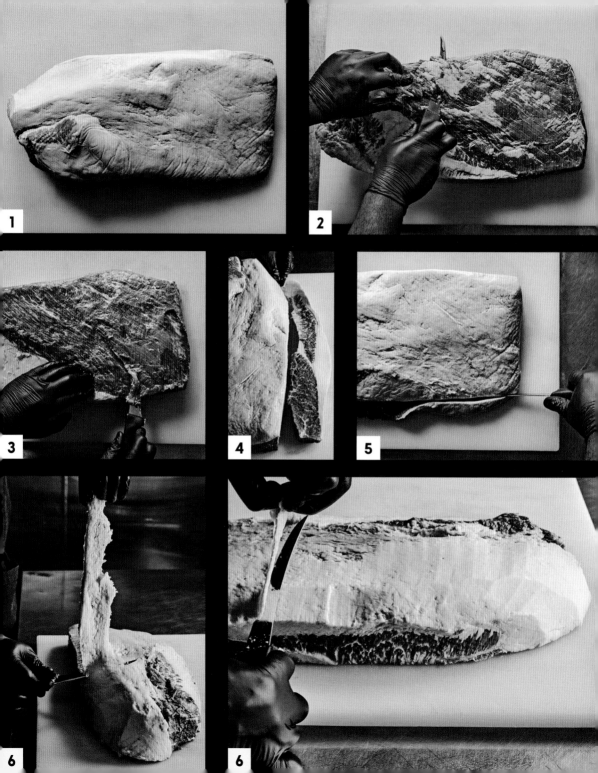

HOW TO
PREPARE HORN BRISKET.

Full recipe follows on page 91.

1. Untrimmed brisket.
2. Trimming the silver skin from the bottom of the brisket.
3. Trimmed bottom of the brisket.
4. Trimming excess fat from the brisket.
5. Trimming fat from and shaping the brisket.
6. Trimming the fat to a ¼-inch (0.6 cm) thickness.
7. Applying mustard bind to the bottom of the brisket.
8. Applying rub to the bottom of the brisket.
9. Applying mustard bind to the top of the brisket.
10. Applying rub to the top of the brisket.

7

8

9

10

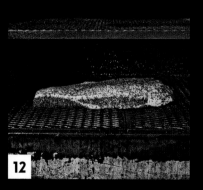

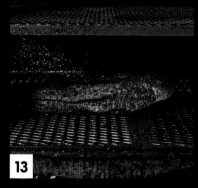

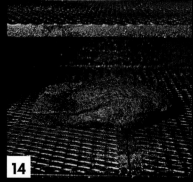

15

16

16

16

11. Raw seasoned brisket before it goes in the smoker.
12. Uncooked brisket.
13. Brisket halfway through the cook.
14. Brisket ready to wrap.
15. Brisket right before pulling from the oven to wrap.
16. Wrapping the brisket.
17. Finished brisket.

17

HORN BRISKET *recipe on page 91.*

This is my signature recipe—the one I spent hours—days—weeks— perfecting to its current juicy goodness. Time is the most important ingredient in this dish, time to let the meat's internal temperature rise to 203°F (95°C). Don't worry about the "stall" (see page 54). Just wait it out and enjoy your smoked masterpiece when it is ready.

YIELD: SERVES 10

PREP TIME: 30 MINUTES

COOK TIME: 7 TO 9 HOURS, PLUS 1 HOUR TO REST

HORN BRISKET

1. Preheat the smoker to 265°F (129°C). I use oak for this cook, but you can use whatever hardwood you can get your hands on.
2. Place the brisket on a work surface so the fatty side is underneath. Trim away any silver skin or excess fat from the brisket and flip the brisket over, fat side facing up. Ideally, you want to keep about ¼-inch (0.6 cm) layer of fat all over the brisket to act as a protective barrier during the long cook.
3. In a small bowl, stir together the pepper, salt, and onion powder (if using). Rub the brisket with mustard or olive oil and apply the seasoning evenly over all sides of the brisket.
4. Place the brisket in the smoker with the point side (thicker side) facing the fire box. Close the lid and don't open it for 6 to 8 hours, or until the internal temperature reaches 165°F (74°C).
5. Spread unwaxed butcher's paper on your work surface, remove the brisket from the smoker, and place it in the middle of the paper. Wrap the brisket until it is completely covered and fold the paper over twice, with the brisket ending right-side up (the side with the fat cap). Place the wrapped brisket back in the smoker, right-side up, and do not remove it until the brisket reaches an internal temperature of 203°F (95°C). The time to achieve this temperature will vary. Pay attention to the feel of the wrapped brisket. As it begins to soften, began probing the brisket to get an idea where the temperature is.
6. Let the wrapped brisket rest, wrapped, for 1 hour before unwrapping it to slice and serve.

1 (12- to 14-pound, or 5 to 6 kg) whole packer brisket

5 tablespoons (30 g) coarse black pepper

2 tablespoons (36 g) coarse kosher salt

2 tablespoons (14 g) onion powder (optional)

Mustard or olive oil, for the meat

This is not a smoker recipe, as the name implies. These succulent ribs are baked in a medium-temperature oven until almost fall-off-the-bone tender. Baby back ribs are leaner than spareribs, and often more expensive, but easier to cut into individual ribs when cooking is complete. Baby back ribs have slightly less flavor than the other rib cuts, so they are usually served with a generous layer of sauce.

OVEN
BABY BACK RIBS

3 tablespoons (54 g)
kosher salt

3 tablespoons (18 g)
coarse black pepper

3 tablespoons (27g)
garlic powder

3 tablespoons (21 g)
onion powder

3 tablespoons (25 g) paprika

2 to 2½ pounds (908 g to 1 kg)
baby back pork ribs

Olive oil or mustard,
for the ribs

1 cup (250 g)
Sweet Barbecue Sauce
(page 206)

1. Preheat the oven to 375°F (190.5°C, or gas mark 5).
2. In a small bowl, stir together the salt, pepper, garlic powder, onion powder, and paprika until well blended.
3. Spread a thin layer of olive oil or mustard over the ribs and season all sides with the rub. Place the ribs in a roasting pan and cover with aluminum foil.
4. Bake for 3 hours, remove from the oven, and coat generously with the barbecue sauce. Re-cover the pan with foil, which allows the sauce to set on the ribs, while the foil cover introduces moisture.
5. Place the sauced ribs back into the oven and bake for 15 minutes, or until they reach an internal temperature of 180°F to 195°F (82°C to 90.5°C) and the meat easily separates from the bone.
6. Let the ribs rest—they will be very hot—until they are cool enough to eat, but still warm. Cut the ribs into individual portions and enjoy!

This is decidedly not a dairy product, but it sets up firmly in a loaf pan and can be sliced like cheese, hence the name. I would probably call this dish a terrine more than anything else, and it is a staple in the Deep South. The pork head is an ingredient you might have to special order from a reputable butcher.

HOG HEAD CHEESE

1. In a 6-quart (6 L) slow cooker, combine the pork head, tongue, carrots, celery, onion, garlic, herbs, spices, and water. Cover the cooker and place it over low heat. Cook for 20 to 24 hours until the meat is thoroughly cooked.
2. Carefully transfer the cooked meat to a large bowl.
3. Strain the broth from the slow cooker through a fine-mesh sieve set over a medium saucepan. Discard the solids. Place the saucepan over medium heat and bring the liquid to a simmer. Simmer for about 30 minutes until the liquid is reduced to 4 cups (960 ml).
4. While the broth simmers, pick the meat from the head and tongue and discard the refuse. Press the meat through a colander to collect the juices and add the juices to the saucepan. Place the meat in a large bowl.
5. Coat a 9 × 5-inch (23 × 13 cm) loaf pan or terrine mold with butter.
6. Shred the meat using two forks and then mix in the reduced broth. Press the meat mixture into the prepared pan. Cover and refrigerate overnight.
7. To unmold, run a knife around the inside edge of the pan, then dip the bottom of the pan in hot water for a few seconds.
8. Invert the head cheese onto a plate or wooden board and garnish with fresh greens.

1 (7-pound, or 3 kg) pork head, cut into 2 or 3 pieces

1 pound (454 g) pork tongue

2 carrots, cut into chunks

2 celery stalks, cut into chunks

1 onion, cut into 8 wedges

5 garlic cloves, skin on, smashed

3 oregano sprigs

3 rosemary sprigs

2 thyme sprigs

5 bay leaves

12 whole allspice berries

12 whole juniper berries

2 cinnamon sticks

1 tablespoon (8.5 g) whole peppercorns

1 tablespoon (18 g) kosher salt

1 teaspoon whole cloves

6 cups water (1 L)

Butter, for preparing the pan

Fresh greens, for garnish

HOW TO

PREPARE BEEF RIBS.

Full recipe follows on page 98.

1. Seasoning the back of the beef ribs.
2. Applying mustard bind to the top of the beef ribs.
3. Spraying the beef ribs midway through the cook to keep them moist.
4. Finished beef ribs.

BEEF RIBS *recipe on page 98.*

Beef ribs might remind you of something a character in a prehistoric cartoon might eat—especially if you usually eat the smaller pork ribs. But cattle are massive animals, so their ribs are an impressive size. This recipe uses five simple ingredients to create culinary magic— succulent, perfectly seasoned beef with a satisfying smoky finish.

BEEF RIBS

¾ cup (180 ml) water

¼ cup (60 ml) vinegar

4½ pounds (2 kg) beef ribs
in a single plate/rack

2 teaspoons kosher salt

2 to 4 tablespoons (24 to 48 g)
Horn Rub (page 217)

Mustard or olive oil,
for the meat

1. Preheat the smoker to 300°F (149°C).
2. Combine the water and vinegar in a spray bottle and set aside.
3. If your beef ribs have a cap still attached, use a sharp knife to remove it, but leave the membrane on the bones intact. Pat the ribs dry with paper towel.
4. Rub mustard or olive oil onto the surface of the meat. Season each side of the ribs with salt, then apply the rub liberally. Massage the seasonings into the meat to ensure it's well coated.
5. Place the rack, meat-side up, in the smoker and smoke for 2 hours.
6. Once the rack has smoked for at least 2 hours, spritz it with the vinegar mixture. Cook for 6 hours more, spritzing the meat every hour or so thereafter, until an instant-read thermometer registers 206°F to 210°F (97°C to 99°C) at the thickest part of the meat. Be careful not to touch the bone with the thermometer when taking a reading as this will give you an inaccurate result.
7. Once at temperature, remove the rack and wrap it in unwaxed butcher's paper, then set the meat in the refrigerator to rest for 1 hour. If you do not have butcher's paper, use aluminum foil, but your bark will soften.
8. Slice the ribs between the bones to serve.

You might not know that meat loaf comes out incredibly flavorful when smoked instead of baked—infused to the last bit with smoky flavor. This meat loaf has a brisket base, so it is the ideal balance of fat and lean that is required for juicy slices. The sticky barbecue sauce glaze takes this recipe over the top. I look forward to a couple cold slices the next day on a sandwich—if there is any leftover.

YIELD: SERVES 3 TO 4

PREP TIME: 15 MINUTES

COOK TIME: 3 HOURS

MEAT LOAF

1. Preheat the smoker to 250°F (121°C). You can use different types of wood (hickory, pecan, maple, mesquite). I use oak for this smoke.
2. In a large bowl, combine the ground brisket, onion, red and green bell peppers, garlic, egg, ⅓ cup (83 g) of barbecue sauce, bread crumbs, salt, black pepper, and cayenne. Use your hands to knead the mixture until everything is completely combined.
3. Mold the meat into a log shape and sprinkle it with the rub.
4. Place the meat loaf in the smoker and smoke for 2 hours.
5. Brush with the remaining ⅓ cup (83 g) of barbecue sauce and cook for about 1 hour more, or until the internal temperature reaches 160°F (71°C).
6. Remove and serve.

2 pounds (908 g) lean brisket, ground

1 onion, chopped

1 red, yellow, or orange bell pepper, chopped

1 green bell pepper, chopped

1 tablespoon (10 g) minced garlic

1 large egg, lightly beaten

⅔ cup (166 g) Sweet Barbecue Sauce (page 206), divided

½ cup (55 g) bread crumbs

1 teaspoon salt

½ teaspoon freshly ground black pepper

¼ teaspoon cayenne pepper

3 tablespoons (36 g) Horn Rub (page 217)

Turkey does not play a starring role in the great Southern barbecue traditions, but it is in fact a pretty common BBQ meat there—and elsewhere—both because there have always been plenty of wild turkeys to hunt and because turkey traditionally has been an inexpensive meat to buy from the supermarket. Three pounds (1 kg) is the size of a typical one-half (one side) turkey breast; if you need to feed more people, just buy both sides and double the rub quantities.

YIELD: SERVES 4

PREP TIME: 15 MINUTES

COOK TIME: 1¼ TO 1½ HOURS

SMOKED TURKEY BREAST

1. Mix the rub ingredients together in a small bowl.
2. Season the turkey breast firmly with the rub and let it sit for up to 1 hour to absorb the flavors.
3. Preheat the smoker to 300°F (149°C) using white oak or your own wood preference.
4. Place the turkey breast in the smoker. Cook the turkey breast until it reaches an internal temperature of 165°F to 170°F (74°C to 77°C), about 1¼ to 1½ hours.

FOR THE RUB

3 tablespoons (14.4 g) ground rosemary

1 teaspoon kosher salt

1 tablespoon (6 g) coarse ground black pepper

1 tablespoon (7 g) smoked paprika

1 teaspoon granulated garlic

1 3-pound (1 kg) turkey breast

OXTAILS *recipe on page 104.*

While I was growing up, my mother would make a bunch of dishes that were inspired by her Southern upbringing, and oxtails was one of those dishes. I would stand in the kitchen the whole time asking my mother when dinner would be ready and she would always respond, "In a little bit." The oxtails would be braised and served with a thick gravy. Smoking oxtails (from cows today, not oxen) is an ideal preparation because they are packed with bone and cartilage with a small ring of meat. The taste might be reminiscent of short ribs as you dig in.

OXTAILS

5 pounds (2 kg) beef oxtails, cut and trimmed

2 tablespoons (30 ml) olive oil

1 tablespoon (18 g) kosher salt

1 tablespoon (9 g) garlic powder

2 teaspoons onion powder

2 teaspoons coarse black pepper

1. Make sure that the oxtails are clean and dry.
2. Place the oxtails on a flat surface and drizzle the olive oil over them.
3. In a small bowl, stir together the salt, garlic powder, onion powder, and pepper until well blended. Generously sprinkle the seasoning all over the oxtails.
4. Place the oxtails in a large freezer bag and refrigerate them overnight.
5. Preheat the smoker to 300°F (149°C).
6. Place the oxtails in the smoker and smoke for 3 to 5 hours (depending on their size!) until the meat starts to pull away from the bone.
7. Remove the oxtails from the smoker and cover them with aluminum foil. Let the oxtails sit for 30 minutes (if eating immediately), or refrigerate or freeze them for later use.

BURN BARREL CHICKEN *recipe on page 111.*

Grilled chicken is an excellent humble family dinner, although the marinade in this recipe adds an incredible glaze worthy of a restaurant meal. The brown sugar speeds up caramelization and deepens the flavor of the finished poultry.

BURN BARREL CHICKEN

1. In a medium bowl, whisk the olive oil, brown sugar, garlic, thyme, and rosemary to blend. Generously season the mixture with salt and pepper and whisk to combine. Reserve ¼ cup (60 ml) of the marinade.
2. Add the chicken thighs to the bowl and toss to coat. Refrigerate the chicken to marinate for at least 20 minutes, and up to overnight.
3. Preheat the grill to medium-high.
4. Place the chicken on the grill and cook for about 6 minutes per side, basting with the reserved marinade, until cooked through and the juices run clear.
5. Garnish with parsley before serving.

3 tablespoons (45 ml) extra-virgin olive oil

2 tablespoons (30 g) brown sugar

1 tablespoon (10 g) minced garlic

1 teaspoon dried thyme

1 teaspoon dried rosemary

Kosher salt

Freshly ground black pepper

4 bone-in, skin-on chicken thighs

Chopped fresh parsley, for garnish

MEATS AND BIRDS

YIELD: SERVES 3 TO 4
PREP TIME: 30 MINUTES
COOK TIME: 4 HOURS

The sugar in the molasses combines with the natural fat in the duck skin to create a mahogany color on the finished smoked duck that is so deep, it looks almost burnished. Look for blackstrap molasses for this recipe. Serve with a Classic Slaw (page 134) or Nina's Potato Salad (page 137) to round out the plate.

SMOKED DUCK

1 large duck or
small wild goose

Kosher salt

¼ cup (85 g)
thick molasses

1. Using oak wood, preheat the smoker to between 200°F and 225°F (93°C and 107°C).
2. Season the duck cavity well with salt, then brush the outside of the bird with the molasses. Season the outside of the duck with salt.
3. Place a drip pan in the smoker and place the bird in the smoker over the drip pan.
4. Smoke the bird for 4 hours, basting the duck with molasses occasionally throughout the cook, until the internal temperature reaches 170°F (77°C).
5. Let the bird cool completely, then carve it. Serve the duck cool or at room temperature as a cold cut or appetizer, or carve the breast whole and sear it in a skillet before slicing and serving.

You might have to source these trotters from a local butcher; they aren't the usual cut found in the meat section of the local grocery store. Pig feet are not ordinarily considered to be the main course, but when served with Granny's Potatoes (page 141) and Pickled Red Onions (page 169), you won't leave the table hungry.

YIELD: SERVES 4

PREP TIME: 15 MINUTES

COOK TIME: 3½ HOURS

SMOKED PIG FEET

1. Preheat the smoker to 325°F (163°C).
2. Rinse the feet and place them in a 9 × 13-inch (23 × 33 cm) baking dish or a Dutch oven. Add the water and salt to the pan and cover with aluminum foil or a lid.
3. Place the baking dish in the smoker and cook for 2½ to 3 hours until the feet are very tender but not falling off the bone. Let them cool briefly.
4. Meanwhile, start your grill. Arrange the briquets on one side of the grill or in a pile in the middle, so there's plenty of room on the grill to indirectly cook the trotters. When the briquets have ashed over and are glowing red, arrange the braised trotters on the grill, skin-side down.
5. Grill for 25 to 35 minutes, turning them occasionally to check that the skin isn't burning, until the meat reaches an internal temperature of 145°F (63°C).
6. In a small serving bowl, stir together the honey and hot sauce.
7. Serve immediately with the sauce on the side.

4 to 5 pig feet, halved lengthwise

½ cup (120 ml) water

2 teaspoons salt

1 tablespoon (20 g) honey

2 teaspoons hot sauce

BURNT ENDS *recipe on page 118.*

The crispy, caramelized "burnt" pieces of a smoked brisket are often the best part, in my humble opinion, because the flavor is concentrated and the texture is pleasing. This recipe creates an entire baking tray of crispy pieces, so you don't have to fight with family members to get them. I like to serve these with a thick chunk of generously buttered corn bread to wipe up the sweet sauce.

BURNT ENDS

1 (4-pound, or 2 kg)
brisket point end

Kosher salt

¼ cup (50 g)
Horn Rub (page 217)

1½ cups (375 g)
Bourbon Sauce (page 212)

1 to 2 tablespoons
(20 to 40 g) honey

1. Preheat the smoker to 250°F (121°C).
2. Season the brisket all over with salt, then rub it all over with the rub.
3. Place the brisket into the smoker and cook for about 4 hours, until it reaches an internal temperature of 150°F (65.5°C).
4. Wrap the brisket in aluminum foil, return it to the smoker, and smoke for about 2 hours, until it reaches an internal temperature of 185°F (85°C).
5. Cut the brisket into ¾-inch (2 cm) cubes, discarding any large seams of fat.
6. Place the brisket cubes in a large foil baking tray, pour in the sauce, and stir to coat. Drizzle the honey over the meat and place the tray in the smoker.
7. Increase the temperature of the smoker to 275°F (135°C) and cook the brisket for 2 to 3 hours until the liquid has reduced and caramelized.
8. Serve immediately, or keep warm until ready to serve, otherwise the sugars in the sauce may harden.

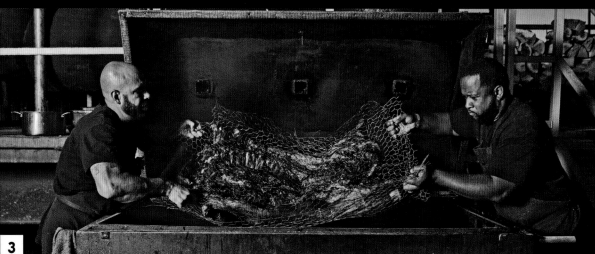

HOW TO PREPARE WHOLE HOG.

Full recipe follows on page 125.

1. Place the hog meat side down, add moisture to the back of the hog, and salt the back.
2. Begin adding coals to the smoker, placing the coals only on the ham side and the shoulder side. Because the belly meat cooks faster, we want to wait until the hog has been flipped before adding coals to the whole hog.
3. Periodically check the hog for color for 8 to 10 hours, depending on the size of your hog. Now it's time to flip the hog. Be careful not to split the center of the hog so you don't lose any moisture during the mopping process.

4

5

6

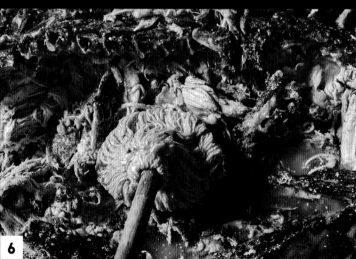

6

4. Once the hog has been flipped, use a spoon to slightly separate the bone and meat. Make sure not to puncture the skin on the hog. This will be important during the mopping process.
5. At this point, begin adding seasoning to the hog.
6. Use your favorite mop and begin mopping the whole hog. This process adds moisture to the meat as it continues to cook on the smoker.
7. Once all the bones and cartilage have been pulled from the meat, begin seasoning and mixing all the meat together.
8. The cracklin.

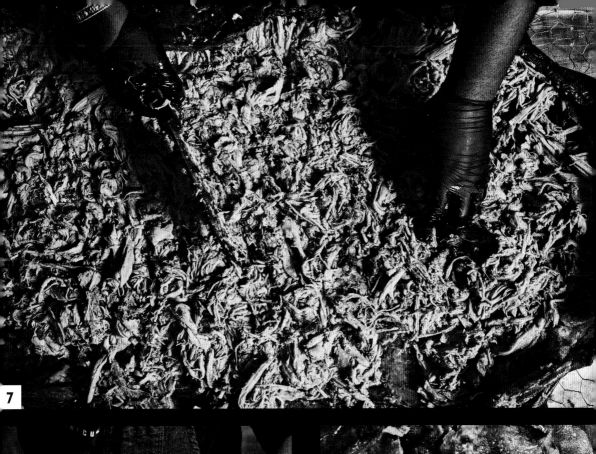

7

7

8

There is something almost medieval about serving up a whole smoked hog, and the feeling of accomplishment is stellar—it takes a whole day to make it happen. Eighty pounds (36 kg) is on the small side for a hog; if your smoker fits a larger hog, go with it. The standard recommendation for determining smoking time is 90 minutes plus 1 hour per pound, but use a thermometer to check for doneness.

YIELD: SERVES 10 TO 12

PREP TIME: 15 MINUTES

COOK TIME: 16 HOURS

WHOLE HOG

1. Prepare a smoker pit with coals from your burn barrel. Preheat the smoker to 275°F (135°C).
2. Lay the hog open so it lies flat, skin-side down. Wet the skin using a rag soaked in water and then cover it with salt. Secure the hog in a stretcher. Set the hog in the smoker, skin-side up. Cook for 6 to 8 hours until the hog reaches an internal temperature of 200°F (93°C), maintaining the smoker temperature and smoke. While maintaining the temperature, fire only the outer perimeter of the hog with coals.
3. At 8 to 10 hours, flip the hog meat-side up. Mop the meat with the sauce and cook until you reach an internal temperature of 200°F (93°C), if you haven't already.
4. Pull the hog from the smoker. Remove all the bones, cartilage, and nodes from the hog. Season to taste and serve.

1 (about 80-pound, or 36 kg) split hog

Kosher salt

1 cup (240 ml) Hog Mop (page 215; depending on the size of your hog, you may have to scale up the mop recipe)

These are going to be the juiciest burgers you've ever had, with a distinct smoky flavor, too. Choose a stronger wood for the burgers because you don't have long to add the smoke flavor. Don't go by the color of the patties to determine when these are done; smoking adds a pink hue to the meat. Look to the internal temperature to ensure a food-safe meal.

SMOKED BURGERS

1¼ pounds (567.5 g) lean (80% lean, 20% fat) ground beef

4 teaspoons Horn Rub (page 217)

4 slices cheddar cheese or your favorite cheese (optional)

4 hamburger buns

Burger toppings of choice

1. Preheat the smoker to 225°F (107°C).
2. Divide the ground beef into four equal portions and shape each into a patty about 4 inches (10 cm) in diameter.
3. Season the patties all over with the rub.
4. Place the patties in the smoker and for about 1 hour, smoke until the internal temperature reaches 140°F (60°C).
5. Increase the temperature to 400°F (204°C) and sear the burgers for about 4 minutes, flipping halfway through the cooking time.
6. Place a slice of cheese on each burger (if using). The patties should be done, 160°F (71°C), at this point.
7. Remove the burgers and toast the buns for a few seconds. Serve the burgers on the buns with your favorite toppings.

This dish is made in the oven, not the smoker, and if you are a fan of oxtails or short ribs, this cut is an inexpensive alternative that is equally delicious. The meat is incredibly tender, and the brown roux creates a rich gravy. I love a thick slice of bread or a bun alongside to soak up all that delicious gravy.

SMOTHERED
NECK BONES

1. Preheat the oven to 375°F (190.5°C, or gas mark 5).
2. Season the neck bones with seasoning salt, pepper, and dried onion and place them in a 9 × 13-inch (23 × 33 cm) roasting pan.
3. Cover the bottom of the roasting pan with ½ inch (1 cm) of water and cover the top of the pan with aluminum foil. Roast for 40 minutes.
4. Using a slotted spoon, transfer the neck bones to a plate. Strain the liquid in the roasting pan through a fine-mesh sieve set over a glass measuring cup to remove any small bones. Discard the solids.
5. Place the roasting pan over medium heat and pour in the oil. Heat until shimmering. Whisk in the flour. Cook for about 4 minutes, whisking constantly, until the flour is golden brown. Add the strained liquid to the roasting pan and whisk to combine.
6. Reduce the oven temperature to 350°F (177°C, or gas mark 4).
7. Return the cooked necks to the roasting pan, re-cover with foil, and cook for 30 minutes until the meat falls off the bones.

8 to 10 beef neck bones

¾ teaspoon seasoning salt

¼ teaspoon freshly ground black pepper

¼ cup (14 g) dried onion

1 tablespoon (15 ml) vegetable oil

½ cup (60 g) all-purpose flour

YIELD: SERVES 4

PREP TIME: 10 MINUTES, PLUS
24 HOURS TO BRINE, 1 HOUR TO
MARINATE, AND 1 HOUR TO REST
AT ROOM TEMPERATURE

COOK TIME:
3 HOURS 30 MINUTES

Rabbit is an incredibly lean meat, so like poultry, it benefits from brining before smoking to keep the meat juicy. This protein is gaining popularity in many areas, so you might get lucky and find it at the grocery store tucked between the lamb and Cornish hens.

SMOKED RABBIT

FOR THE BRINE

¾ cup (180 ml) water

¼ cup (60 ml) dry white wine

1 tablespoon (18 g) kosher salt

1 teaspoon ground black pepper

1 teaspoon garlic powder

1 teaspoon onion powder

FOR THE RUB

1 tablespoon (18 g) kosher salt

1½ teaspoons coarse black pepper

½ teaspoon onion powder

½ teaspoon paprika

½ teaspoon dried oregano

½ teaspoon garlic powder

½ teaspoon dried
parsley flakes

1 (3-pound, or 1 kg)
whole rabbit

TO MAKE THE BRINE

1. In a medium bowl, whisk the water, wine, salt, pepper, garlic powder, and onion powder until well combined. Lay the rabbit flat in a container, pour the brine over it, cover, and refrigerate for 24 hours.

TO MAKE THE RUB

2. In a small bowl, stir together the salt, pepper, onion powder, paprika, oregano, garlic powder, and parsley flakes until well combined.

TO SMOKE THE RABBIT

3. Remove the rabbit from the brine and discard the brine. Rinse the rabbit thoroughly with water and pat it dry with paper towels. Spread the rub all over the rabbit, cover it with plastic wrap, and refrigerate for 1 hour.
4. About 1 hour before smoking, remove the rabbit from the refrigerator and bring it to room temperature.
5. Preheat the smoker to 250°F (121°C).
6. Place the rabbit in the smoker and smoke for 2½ hours.
7. Wrap the rabbit in aluminum foil, return it to the smoker, and smoke for 1 hour until tender.

Lamb is a strongly flavored meat that holds up well to many types of wood. I like oak or hickory for this simple preparation. I especially like preparing this dish to serve to company or to enjoy for Sunday dinner with family. Granny's Potatoes (page 141) and Classic Slaw (page 134) complete the meal.

YIELD: SERVES 6 TO 8

PREP TIME: 15 MINUTES

COOK TIME: 8 HOURS

SMOKED
LAMB SHOULDER

1. Preheat the smoker to 250°F (121°C). Make sure you are burning a clean oxygen-rich fire.
2. In a spritzer bottle, combine the vinegar and apple juice.
3. Rub the lamb all over with the olive oil and season with the rub. Place the lamb in the smoker and smoke for 3 to 3½ hours until a thin bark starts to form.
4. Spritz the lamb with the vinegar mixture. Continue to smoke for about 3 hours more, spritzing the lamb every hour or so with the vinegar mixture, until the lamb reaches an internal temperature of 170°F (77°C), about 6 hours total.
5. Spread unwaxed butcher's paper on your work surface. Place the lamb shoulder in the middle of the paper. Wrap the lamb until it is completely covered and fold the paper over twice. Place the wrapped lamb back in the smoker and do not remove it until it reaches an internal temperature of 203°F (95°C). The time will vary.
6. Let the lamb rest for 30 minutes before pulling the meat from the bones and serving.

½ cup (120 ml) apple cider vinegar

⅓ cup (80 ml) unsweetened apple juice

1 (4- to 5-pound, or 1.8 to 2 kg) bone-in lamb shoulder

1½ tablespoons (23 ml) olive oil

3 tablespoons (36 g) Horn Rub (page 217)

MEATS AND BIRDS

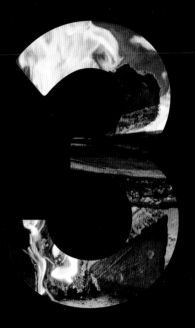

SIDES

SIDES ARE

often considered to be an afterthought, something you throw together to create a complete meal. Not when it comes to barbecue. Don't get me wrong—proteins certainly have that "wow" factor, especially because many take all day, or at least hours, to cook. But the sides I grew up with—many found in this chapter—are the product of years, if not decades, of care and attention. Classic Slaw (page 134) has to be cooling and crunchy for spicy ribs, and Nina's Potato Salad (page 137) needs a perfect balance of tart vinegar, creamy mayo, and spices to complement a perfectly smoked brisket. And don't just save these sides to accompany barbecued proteins; try them as stand-alone dishes, and with other meals—I'm looking at you, Mac and Cheese (page 138)!

When you visualize a table loaded with barbecue items, I bet there is a heaping bowl of slaw. Of course there is, and this recipe is a natural side for smoked meats because its creamy, tart-sweet dressing is cooling and cuts through the richness of the barbecue. If you'd like another pop of color, throw in a shredded carrot or two.

CLASSIC SLAW

2 cups (450 g) mayonnaise

⅓ cup (80 ml) apple cider vinegar

3 tablespoons (60 g) honey

2 tablespoons (22 g) yellow mustard

1 to 1½ teaspoons salt

½ to 1 teaspoon freshly ground black pepper

1 teaspoon dried dill

½ head green cabbage, finely shredded

¼ head purple cabbage, finely shredded

5 scallions, white and green parts, chopped

1. In a large bowl, whisk the mayonnaise, vinegar, honey, mustard, salt, and pepper to taste, and dill until well combined.
2. Add the cabbage and scallions and toss to coat. Transfer the slaw to a large, sealed container and refrigerate for up to 4 days.

One of our first—and favorite—Horn side dishes is our potato salad. This is our take on the classic recipe that goes perfectly with barbecue!

YIELD: SERVES 6 TO 8

PREP TIME: 15 MINUTES

COOK TIME: 10 MINUTES

NINA'S POTATO SALAD

1. Place the potatoes in a large saucepan and cover with 2 inches (5 cm) of water. Bring to a boil over high heat, partially cover the pan, turn the heat to low, and simmer for about 8 minutes until the potatoes are just cooked through. Drain the potatoes, rinse in cold water, and set aside.
2. In a large bowl, whisk the mayonnaise, relish, mustard, rub, paprika, garlic powder, onion powder, salt, and pepper until well blended.
3. Add the cooked potatoes, scallion, and eggs and gently mix to coat and combined.

2½ pounds (1 kg) red potatoes, diced

1½ cups (337.5 g) mayonnaise

¼ cup (60 g) relish

1 tablespoon (11 g) mustard

1 teaspoon Horn Rub (page 217)

1 teaspoon smoked paprika

¾ teaspoon garlic powder

¾ teaspoon onion powder

½ teaspoon salt

¼ teaspoon freshly ground black pepper

½ cup (50 g) chopped scallion, white and green parts (from about 4 scallions)

4 large hard-boiled eggs, peeled and chopped

This homemade mac and cheese is gooey, melty, and incredibly addictive. Heavy cream, generous seasonings, and four types of cheese create comfort food perfection. If you have time, add a layer of buttered bread crumbs and bake to a gorgeous golden brown.

MAC AND CHEESE

Butter, for preparing the casserole dish

Salt

1 pound (454 g) dried elbow macaroni

3 cups (720 ml) heavy cream

1½ cups (360 ml) whole milk

¼ cup (32 g) cornstarch

½ cup (120 ml) water

1 cup (115 g) shredded cheddar cheese

½ cup (57.5 g) shredded provolone cheese

½ cup (57.5 g) shredded smoked Gouda cheese

¼ cup (25 g) grated Parmesan cheese

¾ teaspoon garlic powder

¾ teaspoon onion powder

¾ teaspoon Horn Rub (page 217)

½ teaspoon freshly ground black pepper

1. Preheat the oven to 350°F (177°C, or gas mark 4). Lightly grease a 3- to 4-quart (3 to 4 L) casserole dish with butter.
2. Fill a large pot about three-quarters full of water, generously season the water with salt, and bring to a boil over high heat. Add the pasta and cook according to the package instructions until al dente. Drain and transfer the pasta to the prepared casserole dish.
3. In a large saucepan over medium-high heat, combine the cream and milk. Heat just until boiling.
4. While the milk mixture heats, in a small bowl, whisk the cornstarch and water into a slurry.
5. Turn the heat under the milk mixture to medium and whisk in the slurry until the sauce is thick and smooth. Remove the saucepan from the heat and add the cheddar, provolone, Gouda, and Parmesan. Using an immersion blender, blend in the cheese until very smooth.
6. Stir in 1 teaspoon salt, the garlic powder, onion powder, rub, and pepper. Pour the sauce over the pasta and stir to coat.
7. Bake for about 30 minutes until bubbly and golden brown.

You may have had a version of this over the years. It is a variation of a much-loved Campbell's Soup Company cookbook recipe from the 1970s. We use real potatoes instead of frozen hash browns, but make sure you blanch the potato chunks for about 5 minutes and drain them before finishing them perfectly in the casserole.

YIELD: SERVES 8

PREP TIME: 10 MINUTES

COOK TIME: 1 HOUR 5 MINUTES

GRANNY'S POTATOES

1. Preheat the oven to 325°F (163°C, or gas mark 3).
2. In a large saucepan over medium heat, combine the chicken soup and butter. Cook for about 3 minutes until the butter melts.
3. Transfer the soup mixture to a 9 × 13-inch (23 × 33 cm) casserole dish and stir in the sour cream, garlic powder, onion powder, salt, 1½ cups cheddar, and the scallion until well combined.
4. Add the potatoes and stir to coat. Sprinkle the remaining 1½ cups cheddar evenly over the top.
5. Bake, uncovered, for 1 hour until brown around the edges and the cheese is bubbly.
6. Serve.

1 (10½-ounce, or 298 g) can cream of chicken soup

½ cup (1 stick, or 113 g) butter

1 cup (240 g) sour cream

1 teaspoon garlic powder

1 teaspoon onion powder

1 to 1½ teaspoons salt

3 cups (345 g) shredded cheddar cheese, divided

1 cup (100 g) chopped scallion, green parts only (from 2 or 3 bunches)

2 pounds (908 g) russet potatoes, cut into ½-inch (1 cm) chunks, blanched

Collard greens are a member of the same family as cabbage and kale. They are a traditional ingredient in Southern cooking, often accented with bacon.

COLLARDS

2 tablespoons (28 g) butter

8 ounces (225 g) smoked turkey wings

4 cups (960 ml) chicken stock

1 teaspoon Horn Rub (page 217)

5 cups (about 2¼ pounds, or 1 kg) chopped collard greens

1. In the stockpot over medium heat, melt the butter.
2. Increase the heat to high, place the turkey wings in the pot, and sear for 2 to 3 minutes, turning to brown all sides.
3. Pour in the chicken stock and add the rub. Bring the mixture to a boil. Cover the pot, turn the heat to low, and simmer for about 20 minutes until the meat is falling off the bones.
4. Remove the turkey wings from the stockpot and take all the meat off the bones; discard the bones.
5. Return the meat to the pot and add the collards. Increase the heat under the pot to medium-low and simmer for about 45 minutes until the collards are very tender.

This is such a light summer salad to freshen your palate between barbecue dishes. If you have time, I recommend chilling the salad for about 20 minutes before serving for the best flavor and most refreshing bite.

YIELD: SERVES 4

PREP TIME: 25 MINUTES

WATERMELON SALAD

1. In a large bowl, toss together the watermelon, mint, basil, olives, olive oil, and balsamic vinegar until well mixed.
2. Top with the feta cheese just before serving.

6 cups (900 g) diced watermelon

¼ cup (24 g) chopped fresh mint

¼ cup (10 g) chopped fresh basil

¼ cup (25 g) sliced pitted Kalamata olives

Drizzle olive oil

Drizzle balsamic vinegar

½ cup (75 g) feta cheese

This medium-size legume is another staple ingredient found in traditional barbecue side dishes. Unlike some other beans, black-eyed peas retain their shape, even when simmered to a tender turn. This creates the perfect texture to pair with chunks of smoked turkey—you get a bit of each in every bite.

BLACK-EYED PEAS

1 pound (454 g) dried black-eyed peas, rinsed and picked through

1½ tablespoons (23 ml) olive oil

1 onion, chopped

1 tablespoon (10 g) minced garlic

1 to 2 cups (140 to 280 g) chopped smoked turkey

6 cups (1 L) chicken stock, plus more as needed

Red pepper flakes, for seasoning

1. Place the beans in a stockpot and add enough cold water to cover them with 3 to 4 inches (7.5 to 10 cm). Cover the pot and let sit for 2 to 3 hours. Drain and rinse.
2. Place the now-empty stockpot over medium-high heat, pour in the olive oil, and let it heat. Add the onion and garlic and sauté for about 3 minutes until softened.
3. Add the black-eyed peas, smoked turkey, and enough chicken stock to cover by about 1½ (3.5 cm) inches. Cover the pot and bring the mixture to a boil. Turn the heat to low and simmer for about 1 hour until the black-eyed peas are tender.
4. Remove the stockpot from the heat and let sit, covered, for 15 minutes.
5. Season with red pepper flakes and serve.

This cabbage is more braised than fried, but the smoked sausage adds yummy fat and a "fried" flavor to the veggies. Don't be alarmed by the volume of raw cabbage here. It shrinks down by more than half when cooked—you won't be cooking for an army.

SOUTHERN FRIED CABBAGE

4 smoked andouille sausage links, chopped

1 medium onion, chopped

1 medium red bell pepper, seeded and chopped

2 teaspoons minced garlic

1 head green cabbage, chopped

4 cups (960 ml) chicken stock

1 teaspoon Horn Rub (page 217)

1. In a large pot over medium-high heat, sauté the sausage for about 5 minutes until browned. Using a slotted spoon, transfer the sausage to a plate, leaving any fat behind in the pot.
2. Add the onion, bell pepper, and garlic to the pot. Sauté for about 4 minutes until softened, scraping up any browned bits from the bottom of the pot with a wooden spoon.
3. Add the cabbage, chicken stock, and rub. Cover the pot and bring to a boil. Turn the heat to low and simmer the cabbage for about 40 minutes until tender.
4. Return the sausage to the pot and cook for a few minutes to warm it.
5. Serve.

Red beans and rice is a signature Louisiana Creole dish traditionally made with leftovers like beans, pork, and vegetables. You will be making everything fresh here, but all those classic ingredients are in the pot. Serve heaping spoonfuls over hot, fragrant basmati rice as a side or filling main course.

YIELD: SERVES 6

PREP TIME: 15 MINUTES

COOK TIME: 1 HOUR

MATT'S RED BEANS AND RICE

1. In a large saucepan, combine the water and rice and cook according to the package instructions. Set aside, covered.
2. In a stockpot over medium-high heat, heat the vegetable oil. Add the sausage and sauté for about 4 minutes until browned. Using a slotted spoon, transfer the sausage to a plate, leaving any fat behind in the pan.
3. Add the celery, green pepper, onion, and garlic to the pan. Sauté for about 4 minutes until softened.
4. Stir in the tomato paste and seasoning and sauté for 1 minute until fragrant.
5. Stir in the sausage and any juices on the plate, red beans, chicken stock, bay leaf, and hot sauce to taste. Season with salt and pepper. Bring to a boil, cover the pan, and turn the heat to low. Simmer for 15 minutes.
6. Uncover the pan and simmer for 15 minutes until the beans are soft. Remove the pot from the heat. Using a wooden spoon, mash the beans until thickened.
7. Serve immediately, topped with the rice and parsley.

2 cups (480 ml) water

1 cup (200 g) basmati rice

1 tablespoon (15 ml) vegetable oil

1 (13-ounce, or 368.5 g) package smoked andouille sausage, thinly sliced

3 celery stalks, chopped

1 green pepper, seeded and diced

1 onion, chopped

1 tablespoon (10 g) minced garlic

3 tablespoons (48 g) tomato paste

1½ teaspoons Cajun seasoning

3 (15-ounce, or 425 g) cans red beans, drained and rinsed

3 cups (720 ml) chicken stock

1 bay leaf

Splash hot sauce

Kosher salt

Freshly ground black pepper

3 tablespoons (12 g) chopped fresh parsley

SIDES

149

This Cajun dish is a fusion of many cuisines, such as French, Spanish, and West African, and is the perfect recipe to use up leftover smoked chicken and sausage. If you want to create a Creole version, add chopped tomatoes or a couple tablespoons (about 33 g) of tomato paste. Either way is delicious, and both are fit for company.

JAMBALAYA

8 ounces (225 g) pork or sirloin, cut into small chunks

8 ounces (225 g) smoked andouille sausage, sliced

1 white onion, chopped

1 small green bell pepper, seeded and chopped

1 small red bell pepper, seeded and chopped

1 small yellow bell pepper, seeded and chopped

2 celery stalks, chopped

1 teaspoon minced garlic

4 cups (960 ml) chicken stock

2 cups (400 g) white rice

1 tablespoon (15 ml) Kitchen Bouquet

1½ teaspoons hot Cajun seasoning

1½ teaspoons Creole seasoning (such as Tony Chachere)

1½ teaspoons Accent seasoning

8 ounces (225 g) smoked chicken, chopped

1. In a stockpot over medium-high heat, sauté the pork for about 4 minutes to get rid of the pink. Using a slotted spoon, transfer the pork to a plate.
2. Add the sausage to the pot and sauté for about 4 minutes until lightly browned. Using a slotted spoon, transfer the sausage to the plate with the pork.
3. Add onion; green, red, and yellow bell peppers; celery; and garlic to the pot and sauté for about 5 minutes until softened.
4. Drain the juices out of the pot and return the pork and sausage to the pot.
5. Pour in the chicken stock. Stir in the rice, Kitchen Bouquet, and Cajun, Creole, and Accent seasonings.
6. Bring the jambalaya to a boil. Turn the heat to low and simmer for 30 to 35 minutes until the rice is tender and the liquid is absorbed.
7. Stir in the smoked chicken and heat for a few minutes to warm before serving.

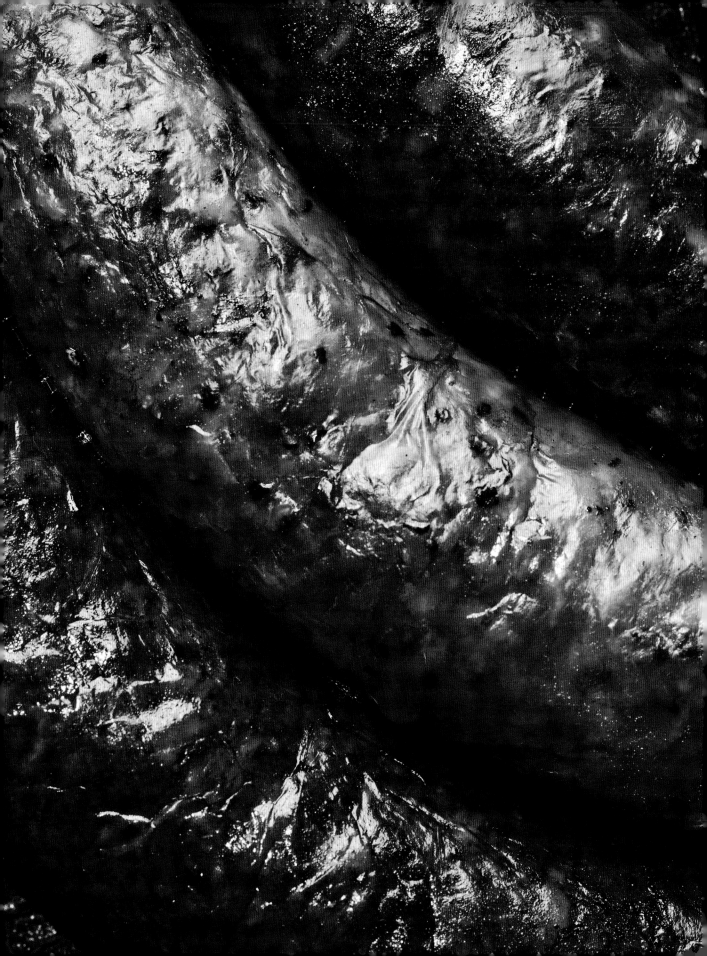

If you celebrate holidays with family, candied yams are likely to make an appearance during a festive meal. This is a toned-down version of this dessertlike dish; some variations add toppings, like chopped pecans and even marshmallows. Serve with turkey, chicken, and a juicy smoked pork butt.

YIELD: SERVES 6 TO 8

PREP TIME: 15 MINUTES

COOK TIME: 1 HOUR

CANDIED YAMS

1. Preheat the oven to 350°F (177°C, or gas mark 4).
2. Arrange the yams in a 9 × 13-inch (23 × 33 cm) baking dish.
3. In a medium saucepan over medium heat, melt the butter.
4. Add the granulated sugar, brown sugar, cinnamon, nutmeg, cloves, and ginger to the butter and cook for about 2 minutes, stirring, until the sugars dissolve.
5. Remove from the heat and stir in the vanilla. Pour the sugar mixture over the yams to coat. Cover the dish with aluminum foil.
6. Bake the yams for 30 minutes. Remove the yams from the oven and baste them with the syrup in the pan. Re-cover the pan and bake for 15 to 20 minutes until caramelized.
7. Remove the yams from the oven and let sit for about 10 minutes before serving.

5 medium-size yams, peeled and cut into ½-inch (1 cm) slices

½ cup (1 stick, or 113 g) salted butter

1 cup (200 g) granulated sugar

¼ cup (60 g) packed brown sugar

1 teaspoon ground cinnamon

½ teaspoon ground nutmeg

¼ teaspoon ground cloves

¼ teaspoon ground ginger

1 tablespoon (15 ml) vanilla extract

Collards make an appearance in this incredibly flavorful recipe; these robust greens are ideal for slow cooking because they hold their texture. Smoked sausage, bacon, veggies, aromatics, and a generous spoon of Horn Rub (page 217) combine with the beans and greens to create a family favorite in my home and, I hope, yours, too.

BEANS AND GREENS

1 pound (454 g) dried black-eyed peas, rinsed and picked through

4 or 5 thick bacon slices, chopped

1 cup (150 g) diced smoked sausage

1 large onion, diced

1 celery stalk, diced

2 to 3 teaspoons minced garlic

1 jalapeño pepper, seeded and chopped

2 teaspoons minced fresh thyme

2 bay leaves

7 to 8 cups (1.7 to 1.9 L) chicken stock or water, plus more as needed

1 to 2 teaspoons Horn Rub (page 217)

Sea salt

2 to 3 cups (140 to 210 g) collard greens

Freshly ground black pepper

Cooked rice, for serving

Sliced scallion, white and green parts, for garnish

1. Place the black-eyed peas in a stockpot and add enough cold water to cover by 3 to 4 inches (7.5 to 10 cm). Cover the pot and let sit for 2 to 3 hours. Drain and rinse.
2. In a large heavy skillet over medium-high heat, sauté the bacon for about 4 minutes until brown and crispy. Add the sausage and sauté for 2 to 3 minutes. Using a slotted spoon, transfer the bacon and sausage to a plate, leaving any fat behind in the skillet.
3. Add the onion, celery, garlic, jalapeño, thyme, and bay leaves to the skillet and sauté for 3 to 4 minutes until the onion is softened.
4. Pour in the chicken stock and stir in the black-eyed peas, rub, and salt. Bring to a boil. Turn the heat to low and simmer, uncovered, for 20 minutes.
5. Add the collard greens, bacon, and sausage and cook for about 10 minutes, stirring occasionally, or until the peas are tender and the mixture is slightly thickened to your liking. Add more stock, or water, if the mixture becomes dry and thick. The texture of the beans should be thick, somewhat creamy but not watery.
6. Remove and discard the bay leaves. Taste and season with pepper and more salt if needed.
7. Serve over cooked rice and garnish with sliced scallion.

YIELD: SERVES 6 TO 8

PREP TIME: 15 MINUTES

COOK TIME: 1 HOUR 15 MINUTES

SOUTHERN GREEN BEANS

1. In a large saucepan over medium heat, sauté the bacon for 6 to 8 minutes, until brown and just cooked through. Add the onion and garlic and sauté for about 4 minutes until softened. Using a slotted spoon, transfer the mixture to a plate, leaving behind any fat in the pan.
2. Place the pan back on the heat and add the green beans, chicken stock, and rub (if using). Bring to a boil. Cover the pan, turn the heat to low, and simmer for 1 hour, stirring occasionally.
3. Drain the broth and stir the bacon mixture into the beans. Cook over medium heat for 1 minute.
4. Stir in the butter and serve.

5 bacon slices, chopped

1 onion, chopped

2 teaspoons minced garlic

2 pounds (908 g) fresh green beans, trimmed

2½ to 3 cups (600 to 720 ml) chicken stock

1 teaspoon Horn Rub (page 217; optional)

2 tablespoons (28 g) butter

Canned beans cut the cook time here, and the added cooked brisket creates a rich taste usually only achieved with hours and hours of baking. I recommend using Sweet Barbecue Sauce (page 206) or Spicy Barbecue Sauce (page 207), depending on your taste preference.

SMOKED PIT BEANS

1 (15-ounce, or 425 g) can pinto beans, drained and rinsed

1 (15-ounce, or 425 g) can kidney beans, drained and rinsed

2 cups (500 g) Sweet Barbecue Sauce (page 206) or Spicy Barbecue Sauce (page 207)

½ cup (120 ml) chicken stock

6 ounces (170 g) cubed cooked brisket

1 teaspoon garlic powder

1 teaspoon onion powder

1 teaspoon salt

½ teaspoon freshly ground black pepper

½ teaspoon Horn Rub (page 217)

1. Preheat the oven to 350°F (177°C, or gas mark 4).
2. In a 9 × 13-inch (23 × 33 cm) baking dish, stir together the pinto beans, kidney beans, barbecue sauce, chicken stock, brisket, garlic powder, onion powder, salt, pepper, and rub to combine. Cover the dish with aluminum foil.
3. Bake for about 1 hour until bubbly and glazed.

Our family loves to get together for Sunday brunch and enjoy this dish. This is our take on a classic New Orleans favorite.

SHRIMP AND GRITS

FOR THE GRITS

2½ cups (600 ml) water

¾ cup (120 g) stone-ground grits

¾ cup (180 ml) milk, plus more as needed

2½ tablespoons (35 g) butter

¾ cup (75 g) grated Parmesan cheese

Sea salt

Freshly ground black pepper

TO MAKE THE GRITS

1. In a large saucepan over high heat, bring the water to a boil. Add the grits, cover the pan, turn the heat to low, and simmer for 15 minutes, stirring often.
2. Pour in the milk. Simmer the grits for about 10 minutes, stirring, until they reach your desired texture. Remove from the heat and stir in the Parmesan and butter. Season with salt and pepper and keep the grits warm while making the shrimp.

TO MAKE THE SHRIMP

3. Place the shrimp in a medium bowl and toss with half the hot sauce and half the Creole seasoning. Cover with plastic wrap and refrigerate.

4. In a large skillet over medium heat, heat 1 tablespoon (15 ml) of olive oil. Toss the reserved shrimp shells into the skillet and cook for about 4 minutes until heated through. Add the remaining hot sauce and Creole seasoning, garlic, and smoked paprika and sauté for 1 minute.

5. Pour in the wine, chicken stock, Worcestershire sauce, and lemon juice. Add the bay leaf and bring the mixture to a simmer. Turn the heat to low and simmer for 12 to 15 minutes until the sauce is reduced by half. Strain the sauce through a fine-mesh sieve set over a heatproof bowl and discard the bay leaf and shells.

6. Place the skill over medium-high heat and pour in the remaining 2 tablespoons (30 ml) of olive oil to heat.

7. Add the shrimp and sauté for about 3 minutes until just cooked through.

8. Pour in the sauce and toss the shrimp to coat. Cook for about 2 minutes until heated through.

9. Remove the skillet from the heat and stir in the butter. Serve the shrimp over the grits and top with parsley.

FOR THE SHRIMP

1 pound (454 g; 21/25 count) jumbo shrimp, peeled and deveined, shells reserved

1½ tablespoons (23 ml) hot sauce, divided

2 teaspoons Creole seasoning, divided

3 tablespoons (45 ml) olive oil, divided

2 teaspoons minced garlic

½ teaspoon sweet smoked paprika

¾ cup (180 ml) dry white wine

3 tablespoons (45 ml) chicken stock

3 tablespoons (45 ml) Worcestershire sauce

Juice of 1 lemon

1 bay leaf

2 tablespoons (28 g) cold butter, chopped

Chopped fresh parsley, for garnish

When I was growing up, we typically ate corn bread with everything. This is our classic corn bread—fluffy and sweet. Pro tip: Bake this bread using your favorite seasoned cast-iron pan.

CLASSIC
CORN BREAD

1. Preheat the oven to 400°F (204°C, or gas mark 6). Lightly coat a 9 × 13-inch (23 × 33 cm) baking dish with butter.
2. In a large bowl, whisk the cornmeal, flour, sugar, baking powder, and salt to blend.
3. In a small bowl, whisk the milk and eggs until blended. Add the milk mixture to the cornmeal mixture and stir until combined. Stir in the melted butter and honey. Pour the batter into the prepared baking dish.
4. Bake for about 25 minutes until the corn bread is lightly browned and a toothpick inserted into the center comes out clean.

½ cup (1 stick, or 113 g) butter, melted, plus more for the baking dish

1½ cups (210 g) cornmeal

1½ cups (180 g) all-purpose flour

⅓ cup (67 g) sugar

1½ tablespoons (21 g) baking powder

1 to 1½ teaspoons salt

1½ cups (360 ml) milk

3 large eggs

¼ cup (80 g) honey

How long does a platter of deviled eggs last at any gathering? Probably about as long as it takes to pull off the plastic wrap covering—they disappear like magic. Pickle juice is the secret ingredient in my version. It adds a "What is that taste?" element that is delightful. Try a little finely chopped bacon or smoked sausage as a delicious topping.

DEVILED EGGS

6 large hard-boiled eggs, peeled and halved

¼ cup (60 g) mayonnaise

1 teaspoon Dijon mustard

1 teaspoon pickle juice

¼ teaspoon salt

¼ teaspoon freshly ground black pepper

¼ teaspoon seasoning salt

Chopped fresh dill, for garnish

1. Using a spoon, carefully scoop the egg yolks from the whites into a medium bowl.
2. Add the mayonnaise, mustard, pickle juice, salt, pepper, and seasoning salt to the yolks and mix until smooth. You can also use a small food processor or an immersion blender to make the filling ultra-smooth.
3. Fill a piping bag fitted with a star tip with the egg yolk mixture. Carefully pipe about 1 tablespoon (15 g) of filling into each egg white half.
4. Garnish with chopped dill and serve immediately, or cover and refrigerate to serve within 24 hours.

Johnny cakes are another name for these fried cornmeal pancakes. For a decadent treat, I love to drizzle them with a bit of honey when serving. If you don't have bacon drippings, try lard instead to get the perfect crispy golden edge.

HOE CAKES

1. In a large bowl, whisk the cornmeal, flour, sugar, and salt until blended.
2. In a small bowl, whisk the buttermilk, water, eggs, and canola oil until combined.
3. Add the wet ingredients to the dry ingredients and whisk until smooth.
4. In a large skillet over medium-high heat, heat the bacon drippings. Working in batches, six to eight cakes per batch, add the batter to the skillet in 2-tablespoon (30 g) measures.
5. Cook until bubbles form on top, flip the cakes over, and cook until the bottom is golden, about 3 minutes total. Transfer the cakes to a plate and repeat with the remaining batter.
6. Serve with butter.

1 cup (140 g) self-rising cornmeal

¾ cup (90 g) all-purpose flour

1½ tablespoons (19 g) sugar

¼ teaspoon salt

⅔ cup (160 ml) buttermilk

⅓ cup (80 ml) water

2 large eggs, beaten

3 tablespoons (45 ml) canola oil

¼ cup (60 ml) bacon drippings

Butter, for serving

PICKLES TO SERVE WITH YOUR 'Q

PICKLES ARE

a Southern tradition—feuds started, marriages planned, and family pride staked on simple Mason jars filled with vegetables and brine. When it comes to barbecue, pickles are essential. The acid and sweetness of pickles cut through the richness of whatever protein is served to create culinary magic. These are a few simple pickles to try your hand; almost any produce can be pickled, so experiment with the bounty of the seasons.

This is a simple pickle that has a distinct heat from the habanero pepper. If you want a more subtle heat, seed the pepper or use a milder variety such as jalapeño. Serve this pretty condiment with Meat Loaf (page 99) or as a flavorful topping on a pulled pork sandwich.

YIELD: MAKES 6
(1-PINT, OR 480 ML) JARS

PREP TIME: 25 MINUTES,
PLUS OVERNIGHT TO REST

COOK TIME: 25 MINUTES

PICKLED
RED ONIONS

1. In a stockpot, combine the vinegar, water, salt, and sugar and bring to a boil over high heat.
2. Stir in the onions and habanero, remove the pot from the heat, cover, and let sit overnight.
3. Place six empty pint-size (480 ml) jars, right-side up, and their lids in a sterilizer rack in another stockpot.
4. Fill the pot and jars with hot water until the jars are covered by 1 inch (2.5 cm) of water. Bring to a boil over medium-high heat and boil for 10 minutes.
5. One at a time, using tongs, remove the hot, sterilized jars and lids and drain.
6. Divide the onions among the sterilized jars and then fill them with the brine. Seal and store in the refrigerator where they will keep for 2 to 3 weeks.

3 cups (720 ml) distilled white vinegar

3 cups (720 ml) water

2/3 cup (192 g) salt

½ cup (100 g) sugar

6 large red onions, thinly sliced

1 habanero pepper, chopped

Okra is a quintessential Southern vegetable that can be an acquired taste because of its reputed "slimy" texture. This characteristic is what makes okra a fantastic thickener in stews and soups. When you pickle okra, it is pleasingly crisp and crunchy, a perfect complement to sticky barbecued ribs. Choose bright green pods about 3 inches (7.5 cm) long for the best results.

PICKLED
OKRA

1 tablespoon (5 g)
coriander seeds

1 tablespoon (6 g)
red pepper flakes

1 tablespoon (11 g)
mustard seeds

1 teaspoon whole
black peppercorns

1 teaspoon celery seeds

1 teaspoon fennel seeds

3 cups (720 ml)
cider vinegar (5% acidity)

2 cups (480 ml) water

2 tablespoons (25 g) sugar

2 tablespoons (36 g)
kosher salt

4 garlic cloves, peeled

1½ pounds (681 g)
fresh okra, trimmed

1. Place four empty pint-size (480 ml) jars, right-side up, and their lids in a sterilizer rack in a stockpot.
2. Fill the pot and jars with hot water until the jars are covered by 1 inch (2.5 cm) of water. Bring to a boil over medium-high heat and boil for 10 minutes.
3. One at a time, using tongs, remove the hot, sterilized jars and lids and drain.
4. In a small bowl, stir together the coriander seeds, red pepper flakes, mustard seeds, peppercorns, celery seeds, and fennel seeds until well mixed. Set aside.
5. In a medium saucepan over medium-high heat, combine the vinegar, water, sugar, and salt and bring to a boil. Cook for about 2 minutes until the sugar dissolves. Turn the heat to low and keep the brine warm.
6. Place one garlic clove into each sterilized jar.
7. Evenly divide the spices among the jars. Pack the okra into the jars and then pour the vinegar mixture over the okra, leaving ¼ inch (0.6 cm) of headspace from the rim of the jar. Run a clean knife between the okra to dislodge any air bubbles. Top up the brine if needed.
8. Screw on the lids, firmly, but not too tight and place the packed jars back in the sterilizer rack in the water. The water should cover the filled jars by about 2 inches (5 cm); add more water if needed. Bring to the boil and let boil for 15 minutes. Remove the rack and let the jars cool—the lids should pop. If the lids do not pop, store the chilled pickles in the refrigerator.
9. Let the pickles sit for 24 hours before eating. If processed correctly (the lids popped), these will last 2 to 3 weeks in the refrigerator, or 1 to 2 months at room temperature.

Pickled green beans have become a trendy addition to cocktails—you may have even spotted mighty jars in your grocery store. I'm here to show you that making pickled green beans at home is so easy, you will never buy them again. The dried chili pepper, cayenne, and peppercorns ensure these crunchy beans pack some heat. If you want a milder bean, cut the amounts of those spices in half.

YIELD: MAKES 4
(1-PINT, OR 480 ML) JARS

PREP TIME: 25 MINUTES

COOK TIME: 25 MINUTES

PICKLED
GREEN BEANS

1. Place four empty pint-size (480 ml) jars, right-side up, and their lids in a sterilizer rack in a stockpot.
2. Fill the pot and jars with hot water until the jars are covered by 1 inch (2.5 cm) of water. Bring to a boil over medium-high heat and boil for 10 minutes.
3. One at a time, using tongs, remove the hot, sterilized jars and lids and drain.
4. In a small bowl, stir together the chili pepper, cayenne, fennel seeds, and peppercorns until well mixed. Set aside.
5. In a medium saucepan over medium-high heat, combine the vinegar, water, and salt and bring to a boil. Cook for about 2 minutes until the salt dissolves. Turn the heat to low and keep the mixture warm.
6. Place one garlic clove into each sterilized jar and evenly divide the spices among the jars.
7. Pack the green beans into the jars and pour the vinegar mixture over the green beans, leaving ¼ inch (0.6 cm) of headspace from the rim of the jar. Run a clean knife between the green beans to dislodge any air bubbles. Top up the brine if needed.
8. Screw on the lids, firmly, but not too tight and place the packed jars back in the sterilizer rack in the water. The water should cover the filled jars by about 2 inches (5 cm); add more water if needed. Bring to the boil and let boil for 15 minutes. Remove the rack and let the jars cool—the lids should pop. If the lids do not pop, store the chilled pickles in the refrigerator.
9. Let the pickles sit for 24 hours before eating. Keep refrigerated for up to 3 weeks.

1 tablespoon (2 g) dried chili pepper

1½ teaspoons cayenne pepper

1 teaspoon fennel seeds

1 teaspoon whole black peppercorns

2 cups (480 ml) apple cider vinegar

2 cups (480 ml) water

2 tablespoons (36 g) kosher salt

4 garlic cloves, peeled

8 ounces (225 g) fresh green beans, trimmed

This is a standard pickle recipe for crisp carrots; the sweetness of this colorful root vegetable is enhanced by the tart-sweet brine and kick of mustard and fennel seeds. If you can get your hands on heirloom carrots—red, yellow, purple, and white—these pickles will look like art. Perfect as a gift from your kitchen or to serve for holiday meals.

PICKLED
CARROTS

1 tablespoon (11 g) mustard seeds

1 teaspoon fennel seeds

1 teaspoon whole black peppercorns

2 cups (480 ml) apple cider vinegar

2 cups (480 ml) water

2 tablespoons (25 g) sugar

2 tablespoons (36 g) kosher salt

4 garlic cloves, peeled

8 ounces (225 g) 2- to 3-inch (5 to 7.5 cm)-long carrots

1. Place four empty pint-size (480 ml) jars, right-side up, and their lids in a sterilizer rack in a stockpot.
2. Fill the pot and jars with hot water until the jars are covered by 1 inch (2.5 cm) of water. Bring to a boil over medium-high heat and boil for 10 minutes.
3. One at a time, using tongs, remove the hot, sterilized jars and lids and drain.
4. In a small bowl, stir together the mustard seeds, fennel seeds, and peppercorns until well mixed. Set aside.
5. In a medium saucepan over medium-high heat, combine the vinegar, water, sugar, and salt and bring to a boil. Cook for about 2 minutes until the sugar dissolves. Turn the heat to low and keep the mixture warm.
6. Place one garlic clove into each sterilized jar and evenly divide the spices among the jars.
7. Pack the carrots into the jars and pour the vinegar mixture over the carrots, leaving ¼ inch (0.6 cm) of headspace from the rim of the jar. Run a clean knife between the carrots to dislodge any air bubbles. Top up the brine if needed.
8. Screw on the lids, firmly, but not too tight and place the packed jars back in the sterilizer rack in the water. The water should cover the filled jars by about 2 inches (5 cm); add more water if needed. Bring to the boil and let boil for 15 minutes. Remove the rack and let the jars cool—the lids should pop. If the lids do not pop, store the chilled pickles in the refrigerator.
9. Let the pickles sit for 24 hours before eating. Keep refrigerated for up to 3 weeks.

This recipe has a reputation of being a Southern creation, but pickled pig feet are popular worldwide. The added spices and seasonings create a complex flavor with the pork rather than the expected vinegar. When you cut the brine with water, the pork flavor still shines through. I like to serve these with a Southern-style green, such as Collards (page 142) or Southern Green Beans (page 155).

YIELD: MAKES 3
(1-PINT, OR 480 ML) JARS

PREP TIME: 25 MINUTES

COOK TIME:
2 HOURS 30 MINUTES

PICKLED
PIG FEET

1. Place three empty pint-size (480 ml) jars, right-side up, and their lids in a sterilizer rack in a stockpot.
2. Fill the pot and jars with hot water until the jars are covered by 1 inch (2.5 cm) of water. Bring to a boil over medium-high heat and boil for 10 minutes.
3. One at a time, using tongs, remove the hot, sterilized jars and lids and drain.
4. Wash the pig feet and place them in another stockpot and add enough water to cover by about 2 inches (5 cm). Bring to a boil over medium-high heat, turn the heat to low, and simmer for about 2 hours, skimming any foam that accumulates on the surface of the water occasionally, until the feet are tender.
5. Using a slotted spoon, remove the feet and rinse them under hot water. Remove as many bones as possible from the feet and set the feet aside.
6. Clean the pot and, in it, combine the vinegar, water, salt, sugar, mustard seeds, fennel seeds, peppercorns, and chili pepper and bring to a boil over medium-high heat. Turn the heat to low and simmer for about 30 minutes.
7. Add the feet to the simmering liquid and bring it to a full boil, then remove the pot from the heat.
8. Using a slotted spoon, transfer the feet to the jars. Place a garlic clove into each jar and pour the pickling liquid over the feet. Secure the lids on the jars. Let cool.
9. Store the jars in the refrigerator for 4 to 7 days before eating.

4 whole pig feet,
halved lengthwise

2 cups (480 ml)
apple cider vinegar

2 cups (480 ml) water

2 tablespoons (36 g)
kosher salt

2 tablespoons (25 g)
granulated sugar

1 tablespoon (11 g)
mustard seeds

1 teaspoon fennel seeds

1 teaspoon whole
black peppercorns

1 tablespoon (2 g)
dried chili pepper

3 garlic cloves, peeled

5

DESSERTS

THE SOUTH IS FAMOUS

for desserts. Iconic and much-loved classics inspire every recipe in this chapter. I will bet each choice conjures a memory of a family gathering, holiday, neighborhood potluck, or church event. You might notice a few include boxed cake mix and pudding options—there are a couple of good reasons for this inclusion. The most important is that the original recipes from family members and friends utilize these ingredients, and although I tweaked the end product, I wanted to stay true to their creations. Number two, these ingredients are incredibly convenient and inexpensive, and the finished desserts are spectacular. Let's dig in.

You would never know this rich dessert was invented centuries ago to use up stale bread that would otherwise be thrown away. This version is extra scrumptious with luscious heavy cream–based custard and flaky, buttery croissants. I love to serve this pudding with sliced fresh strawberries to add a gorgeous pop of color.

BREAD PUDDING

FOR THE BASE

5 cups (1 L) heavy cream

14 large egg yolks

1¼ cups (250 g) sugar

1 tablespoon (15 ml) vanilla extract

FOR THE PUDDING

8 croissants, torn into 1½-inch (3.5 cm) pieces

¼ cup (60 ml) melted butter

TO MAKE THE BASE

1. In a large saucepan over medium heat, warm the cream until just below scalding.
2. In a large bowl, whisk the egg yolks and sugar until blended. Slowly add the warm cream to the egg yolks, whisking constantly. Whisk in the vanilla.

TO MAKE THE PUDDING

3. Preheat the oven to 350°F (177°C, or gas mark 4).
4. Place the torn croissants in a 9 × 13-inch (23 × 33 cm) baking dish, drizzle with the melted butter, and toss to coat and combine. Pour the base over the croissants, toss to coat, and let stand for 15 minutes.
5. Bake for 50 to 55 minutes until golden and a knife inserted into the center comes out clean.

Lemon is one of the most popular dessert flavors. Who doesn't love that tart-sweet delight that perks up the taste buds? Using buttermilk adds a pleasing tanginess and creates a lovely tender crumb texture. If you don't have buttermilk, swap in milk in the same amount with 1½ teaspoons of distilled vinegar stirred in.

LEMON CAKE

FOR THE CAKE

Nonstick cooking spray

1¼ cups (150 g) sifted all-purpose flour, plus more for the pans

⅔ cup (160 ml) vegetable oil

⅓ cup (64 g) vegetable shortening, at room temperature

1½ cups (300 g) granulated sugar

2 teaspoons pure lemon extract

1 teaspoon vanilla extract

3 large eggs

Finely grated zest of 1 large lemon

1½ cups (180 g) sifted cake flour

1½ teaspoons baking powder

1 teaspoon salt

½ teaspoon baking soda

1½ cups (360 ml) buttermilk

TO MAKE THE CAKE

1. Preheat the oven to 350 °F (177°C, or gas mark 4). Coat two (9-inch, or 23 cm) round cake pans with cooking spray and dust them with all-purpose flour, knocking out the excess. Line the bottoms of the pans with two (9-inch, or 23 cm) parchment paper circles.
2. In a large bowl, using an electric mixer, beat the oil, shortening, and granulated sugar until fluffy. Add the lemon extract and vanilla and beat to combine.
3. One at a time, add the eggs, beating well after each and scraping down the sides of the bowl between additions. Fold in the lemon zest.
4. In a medium bowl, sift together the all-purpose and cake flours, baking powder, salt, and baking soda. Add the dry ingredients to the wet ingredients, alternating with the buttermilk in five additions, starting and ending with the flour mixture. Pour the batter evenly into the prepared pans.
5. Bake for 30 to 35 minutes until a toothpick inserted into the center of the cakes comes out clean.
6. Set aside to cool completely.

TO MAKE THE FROSTING

7. In a medium bowl, stir together the confectioners' sugar, butter, and lemon zest (if using) until the mixture becomes crumbly.
8. Stir in the lemon extract and 1 tablespoon (15 ml) milk.
9. Using an electric mixer, beat the frosting until very smooth and fluffy, adding only enough milk to bring the frosting to a creamy, spreadable consistency.
10. Place one cake on a cake board or serving plate. Frost the top of the layer with about ¾ cup of frosting and place the second cake on top. Frost the top and sides of the cake with the remaining frosting.
11. Refrigerate the frosted cake until you are ready to serve.

FOR THE FROSTING

4 cups (448 g)
confectioners' sugar

1 cup (2 sticks, or 226 g) butter

1 teaspoon minced
lemon zest (optional)

1 teaspoon pure lemon extract

2 tablespoons (30 ml) milk

Think of a velvety pound cake drenched in buttery, sweet rum glaze as the dessert centerpiece after a festive meal. Surprisingly light, this golden Bundt cake is the perfect finish for a rib and slaw dinner. Depending on what I have on hand, I like to experiment with different rums to create unique variations.

RUM CAKE

FOR THE CAKE

Nonstick cooking spray

1¾ cups (350 g) sugar plus
2 tablespoons (25 g)

2½ cups (300 g) cake flour

1¼ teaspoons baking powder

1 teaspoon salt

½ teaspoon baking soda

1 cup (2 sticks, or 226 g) butter, melted

6 large egg yolks,
at room temperature

½ cup (120 ml) buttermilk,
at room temperature

½ cup (120 ml) rum

1 tablespoon (15 ml)
vanilla extract

3 large egg whites,
at room temperature

TO MAKE THE CAKE

1. Preheat the oven to 350°F (177°C, or gas mark 4). Coat a 10-inch (30 cm) Bundt pan with cooking spray and then add 2 tablespoons (25 g) sugar, gently tapping and turning the pan to coat the inside.

2. In a large bowl, whisk the cake flour, 1½ cups (300 g) sugar, baking powder, salt, and baking soda until combined.

3. In a medium bowl or glass measuring cup, whisk the melted butter, egg yolks, buttermilk, rum, and vanilla until well blended.

4. In another large bowl, using an electric mixer, beat the egg whites for about 30 seconds until foamy. While beating the egg whites, 1 tablespoon (12.5 g) at a time, add the remaining ¼ cup (50 g) of sugar and continue to beat for 1 to 1½ minutes until stiff peaks just form.

5. Beat the melted butter mixture into the flour mixture on medium-low speed for about 15 seconds until just combined. Scrape the bowl and beat the mixture for about 15 seconds more until smooth. Fold one-quarter of the whipped egg whites into the batter until just combined, then add the remaining whites and gently fold until no white streaks remain. Spoon the batter evenly into the prepared Bundt pan.

6. Bake for 40 to 50 minutes until a toothpick inserted into the center of the cake comes out clean. Transfer the cake to a wire rack and let cool for 15 minutes.

TO MAKE THE BUTTER-RUM SAUCE

7. While the cake cools, in a medium saucepan over medium-high heat, whisk the sugar, butter, and water to combine. Bring to a boil, stirring occasionally, and continue to boil for about 5 minutes until the sugar dissolves.
8. Remove the sauce from the heat and gradually whisk in the rum. Be careful, as the rum will make the sauce boil again.
9. Using a toothpick, poke holes all over the surface of the cake. Pour half the sauce over the cake and let it sit for 15 minutes to absorb the liquid.
10. Carefully invert the cake onto a serving platter and drizzle the remaining sauce over the cake.
11. Serve immediately, or cover until ready to serve.

FOR THE BUTTER-RUM SAUCE

1 cup (200 g) sugar

½ cup (1 stick, or 113 g) butter

¼ cup (60 ml) water

¼ cup (60 ml) rum

YIELD: SERVES 4 TO 6

PREP TIME: 30 MINUTES, PLUS 30 MINUTES TO SET

BANANA PUDDING

1. In a large bowl, whisk the pudding and milk until blended. Refrigerate for about 30 minutes until set.
2. In a medium bowl, whisk the condensed milk and cream cheese until blended. Fold the cream cheese mixture into the pudding.
3. In another medium bowl, using a whisk or an electric mixer, whip the heavy cream for about 4 minutes until soft peaks form. Fold the whipped cream into the pudding mixture and refrigerate.
4. Crush five vanilla wafers for topping and set aside.
5. Arrange ten wafers in the bottom of a 2-quart (2 L) serving bowl. Layer half the pudding and bananas on top of the wafers. Repeat the layers with the remaining ingredients and top with the crushed wafers. Refrigerate until you are ready to serve.

1 (3-ounce, or 96 g) package instant vanilla pudding mix

2 cups (480 ml) cold whole milk

1 (7-ounce, or 200 g) can sweetened condensed milk

½ cup (115 g) cream cheese, at room temperature

1 cup (240 ml) heavy cream

25 vanilla wafer cookies

2 bananas, sliced

DESSERTS

This intensely colored cake is a legend, a classic, a spectacular feast for the eyes when cut into thick slices. If you have never enjoyed red velvet cake, the subtle chocolate flavor paired with tangy cream cheese frosting, I think this cake will delight. Don't omit the buttermilk because it helps create the soft, "velvet" texture and brings out the red anthocyanin found in the cocoa, which enhances the signature color.

RED VELVET CAKE

FOR THE CAKE

Nonstick cooking spray

2½ cups (300 g) cake flour, plus more for the pans

1 cup (2 sticks, or 226 g) butter, at room temperature

1¾ cups (350 g) granulated sugar

2 large eggs

1 tablespoon (15 ml) red food coloring

1 tablespoon (15 ml) distilled white vinegar

2 teaspoons vanilla extract

3 tablespoons (16 g) unsweetened cocoa powder

1 teaspoon salt

1 teaspoon baking soda

1 cup (240 ml) buttermilk

TO MAKE THE CAKE

1. Preheat the oven to 350°F (177°C, or gas mark 4). Coat three (8-inch, or 20 cm) round cake pans with cooking spray and dust them with flour, knocking out the excess.
2. In a large bowl, combine the butter and granulated sugar. Using an electric mixer, beat until fluffy.
3. Add the eggs, food coloring, vinegar, and vanilla and beat until smooth.
4. In a medium bowl, stir together the flour, cocoa powder, salt, and baking soda until blended. Add the dry ingredients to the wet ingredients, alternating with the buttermilk, in five additions, starting and ending with the flour mixture, beating until combined. Pour the batter evenly into the prepared pans.
5. Bake for 20 to 25 minutes until a toothpick inserted into the center of the cakes comes out clean. Set aside to cool completely.

TO MAKE THE FROSTING

6. In a medium bowl, combine the cream cheese and butter. Using an electric mixer, beat until well blended. Add the marshmallow creme and beat until combined. Add the confectioners' sugar and beat until thick and fluffy. Fold in the coconut.

7. Place one cake on a cake board or serving plate. Frost the top of the layer with about 1 cup of frosting and place the second cake on top. Frost the top of that layer with about 1 cup of frosting and place the final cake on top. Frost the top and sides of the cake with the remaining frosting.

8. Refrigerate the frosted cake until you are ready to serve.

FOR THE FROSTING

1 (8-ounce, or 225 g) block cream cheese

½ cup (1 stick, or 113 g) butter, at room temperature

1 cup (104 g) marshmallow creme

3½ to 4 cups (392 to 448 g) confectioners' sugar

1 to 1½ cups (120 to 180 g) shredded sweetened coconut

This is an ode to my dear grandmother, Ms. Elsie Brown. She would always have this cake on a cake stand on her kitchen table, and she would cut me a thick slice and serve it to me with a glass of milk when I'd visit her.

PINEAPPLE UPSIDE-DOWN CAKE

½ cup (1 stick, or 113 g) butter, plus more for the pan

½ cup (120 g) packed brown sugar

1 (14-ounce, or 397 g) can pineapple slices packed in 100 percent juice, drained, juice reserved (up to 1 cup)

Maraschino cherries, for garnish

1 (15-ounce, or 432 g) box French vanilla or yellow cake mix

3 large eggs

½ cup (120 ml) canola oil

1. Preheat the oven to 350°F (177°C, or gas mark 4). Coat a 10-inch (30 cm) Bundt pan with butter.
2. In a small saucepan over low heat, melt the butter. Add the brown sugar and stir until smooth. Pour the mixture evenly into the prepared Bundt pan, tilting it to coat the sides.
3. Blot the pineapple slices dry with a paper towel and arrange them in the bottom of the Bundt pan, not overlapping, but you can squeeze them together if necessary. Place a Maraschino cherry in the center of each ring.
4. In a large bowl, whisk the cake mix, reserved pineapple juice, eggs, and oil until thick and smooth. Carefully pour the batter into the pan.
5. Bake for about 40 minutes until a toothpick inserted into the center of the cake comes out clean.
6. Cool the cake for 15 minutes in the pan, then invert it onto a serving plate. Let the cake cool completely and serve.

This is a statement dessert—three towering layers of cake filled with cream cheese frosting and then completely covered in coconut shreds. The sour cream in the cake balances the sweetness of the frosting. If you want to intensify the coconut flavor, lightly toast the shredded coconut in a large skillet over medium-low heat, stirring constantly, until golden brown.

COCONUT CAKE

FOR THE CAKE

Nonstick cooking spray

All-purpose flour, for the pans

2 (15-ounce, or 432 g) boxes white or yellow cake mix

6 large eggs

1¾ cups (420 g) sour cream

½ cup (120 ml) vegetable oil

1 (15-ounce, or 425 g) can cream of coconut

FOR THE FROSTING

2 (8-ounce, or 225) blocks cream cheese, at room temperature

1 tablespoon (15 ml) vanilla extract

6 to 6½ cups (672 to 728 g) confectioners' sugar

¼ cup (60 ml) whole milk, at room temperature

8 cups (960 g) shredded sweetened coconut

TO MAKE THE CAKE

1. Preheat the oven to 350°F (177°C). Lightly coat three (9-inch, or 23 cm) round cake pans with cooking spray and dust with flour, knocking out the excess.
2. In a large bowl, using an electric mixer, beat the cake mix, eggs, sour cream, vegetable oil, and cream of coconut for about 3 minutes until fluffy.
3. Divide the batter evenly among the prepared cake pans. The pans should be slightly more than half full.
4. Bake for about 30 minutes until a toothpick inserted into the center of the cakes comes out clean.
5. Let cool completely.

TO MAKE THE FROSTING

6. In a large bowl, using an electric mixer, beat the cream cheese and vanilla until very smooth, stopping to scrape down the sides of the bowl with a spatula as needed.
7. Add the confectioners' sugar and beat until completely mixed.
8. Mix in the milk, as needed, to reach a spreadable consistency.

TO ASSEMBLE THE CAKE

9. Frost the top of one cake with about 1 cup (264 g) of frosting and place a second cake on top. Frost the top of that second layer with about another 1 cup (264 g) of frosting and place the final cake on top. Frost the top and sides of the cake with the remaining frosting.
10. Press the coconut into the sides and onto the top of the cake.
11. Refrigerate the frosted cake until you are ready to serve.

Chocolate and coffee are a natural combination—the bitter taste of the coffee enhances the chocolate beautifully. This decadent cake can be whipped together in a flash because you use box cake mix and instant pudding. This doubles the chocolate flavor, and the pudding creates an almost fudge-like moist texture.

YIELD: SERVES 8

PREP TIME: 20 MINUTES

COOK TIME: 55 MINUTES, PLUS 15 MINUTES TO COOL

KAHLÚA CAKE

TO MAKE THE CAKE

1. Preheat the oven to 350°F (177°C, or gas mark 4). Coat a 10-inch (30 cm) Bundt pan with cooking spray and dust it with flour, knocking out the excess.
2. In a large bowl, whisk the cake mix, pudding mix, sugar, eggs, coffee, Kahlúa, and canola oil until blended and thick. Pour the batter into the prepared Bundt pan.
3. Bake for 45 to 50 minutes until a toothpick inserted into the center of the cake comes out clean.

TO MAKE THE GLAZE

4. While the cake bakes, in a small saucepan over low heat, melt the butter. Stir in the sugar and cook for about 4 minutes until it dissolves. Remove the saucepan from the heat and stir in the Kahlúa. Set aside.

TO FINISH THE CAKE

5. Using a toothpick, poke holes all over the cake while it is in the pan. Pour the glaze over the surface, allowing it to soak in.
6. Let the cake cool for 15 minutes, then turn it out onto a serving plate to serve.

FOR THE CAKE

Nonstick cooking spay

All-purpose flour, for the pan

1 (15-ounce, or 432 g) box devil's food chocolate cake mix

1 (3-ounce, or 96 g) box instant chocolate pudding mix

½ cup (100 g) sugar

4 large eggs

¾ cup (180 ml) strong brewed coffee, cooled

½ cup (120 ml) Kahlúa or other coffee-flavored liqueur

½ cup (120 ml) canola oil

FOR THE GLAZE

½ cup (1 stick, or 113 g) butter

1 cup (200 g) sugar

⅓ cup (80 ml) Kahlúa or other coffee-flavored liqueur

Key lime pie is an American classic, so why not combine all those wonderful flavors in a glorious three-tier cake? What exactly is a key lime? Key limes are small, tart, sweet, yellowish, and almost floral-tasting fruits also known as Mexican or West Indies limes. Sourcing them for this tempting cake is worth the effort, but if not available, use the larger Persian limes found in every grocery store.

KEY LIME CAKE

FOR THE CAKE

Nonstick cooking spray

2 cups (240 g) all-purpose flour, plus more for the pans

1¼ cups (250 g) granulated sugar

1 (3-ounce, or 85 g) package lime-flavored gelatin

1 teaspoon baking soda

1 teaspoon baking powder

½ teaspoon sea salt

1½ cups (360 ml) canola oil

5 large eggs

¾ cup (180 ml) fresh orange juice

Juice of ½ lemon

1 teaspoon vanilla extract

TO MAKE THE CAKE

1. Preheat the oven to 350°F (177°C, or gas mark 4). Coat three (9-inch, or 23 cm) round cake pans with cooking spray and dust them with flour, knocking out the excess.
2. In a large bowl, whisk the flour, granulated sugar, gelatin, baking soda, baking powder, and salt until blended.
3. In a medium bowl, whisk the canola oil, eggs, orange juice, lemon juice, and vanilla until combined.
4. Add the wet ingredients to the dry ingredients and whisk until smooth. Divide the batter evenly among the prepared cake pans.
5. Bake for 35 to 40 minutes until a toothpick inserted into the center of the cakes comes out clean.
6. Cool the cakes in the pans for 10 minutes, then turn them out onto a wire rack.

TO MAKE THE LIME GLAZE

7. While the cakes cool, in a small bowl, whisk the lime juice and sugar until well blended.
8. Using a toothpick, poke the still-warm layers all over and pour the glaze evenly over each layer, allowing the liquid to soak into the cakes.
9. Let cool completely.

TO MAKE THE CREAM CHEESE FROSTING

10. In a medium bowl, whisk the cream cheese and butter until blended.
11. Add the confectioners' sugar and whisk until the frosting is smooth and thick.
12. Place one cake layer on a serving plate. Frost the top of the layer with about ¾ cup (198 g) of frosting and place the second cake on top. Frost the top of that layer with about ¾ cup (198 g) of frosting and place the final cake on top. Frost the top and sides of the cake with the remaining frosting.
13. Refrigerate the frosted cake until you are ready to serve.

FOR THE LIME GLAZE

½ cup (120 ml) fresh key lime juice

½ cup (56 g) confectioners' sugar

FOR THE CREAM CHEESE FROSTING

1 (8-ounce, or 225 g) block cream cheese, at room temperature

½ cup (1 stick, or 113 g) butter, at room temperature

3 to 3½ cups (336 to 392 g) confectioners' sugar

Sour cream is an exceptional ingredient for cakes because its high fat content ensures a tender, moist crumb. Look for full-fat sour cream—18 percent, if possible—for the best flavor and texture. Greek yogurt or crème fraîche is an acceptable substitute if you used up all your sour cream making Granny's Potatoes (page 141).

SOUR CREAM CAKE

TO MAKE THE CAKE

1. Preheat the oven to 350°F (177°C, or gas mark 4). Coat a 10-inch (30 cm) Bundt pan with cooking spray and dust it with flour, knocking out any excess.
2. In a large bowl, combine the butter and granulated sugar. Using an electric mixer, beat for about 3 minutes until fluffy, stopping to scrape down the sides with a spatula as needed.
3. One at a time, add the egg yolks, beating well after each addition, until well blended. Beat in the sour cream and vanilla until blended.
4. In a small bowl, whisk the flour, baking soda, and salt until blended. Add the dry ingredients to the wet ingredients and beat until mixed.
5. In a large stainless steel or glass bowl, using an electric mixer, beat the egg whites for about 3 minutes until stiff peaks form.
6. Stir one-quarter of the whipped egg whites into the batter to lighten it. Gently fold in the remaining egg whites until no white streaks remain. Pour the batter into the prepared Bundt pan.
7. Bake for 1 to 1½ hours until a toothpick inserted into the center of the cake comes out clean.
8. Cool the cake in the pan for 20 minutes, then invert the pan carefully onto a rack to turn out the cake.

TO MAKE THE GLAZE

9. In a medium bowl, whisk the cream cheese, butter, and vanilla until blended.
10. Add the confectioners' sugar, whisk until smooth, and pour the glaze over the cooled cake.

FOR THE CAKE

Nonstick cooking spray

3 cups (360 g) all-purpose flour, plus more for the pan

1 cup (2 sticks, or 226 g) butter, at room temperature

2¾ cups (550 g) granulated sugar

6 large eggs, separated, at room temperature

1 cup (240 g) sour cream

1½ teaspoons vanilla extract

½ teaspoon baking soda

¼ teaspoon salt

FOR THE GLAZE

½ cup (115 g) cream cheese, at room temperature

¼ cup (½ stick, or 56 g) butter, at room temperature

1 teaspoon vanilla extract

1 cup (112 g) confectioners' sugar

DESSERTS

197

Did you know National Peach Cobbler Day is April 13? This national day of cobbler celebration began in the 1950s and was created by the Georgia Peach Festival not only to celebrate this homey dessert but also to sell some canned peaches! Cobbler is named for its rough "cobbled together," lightly sweetened biscuit topping. You can enjoy this traditional dessert year-round by substituting canned peaches packed in 100 percent fruit juice.

GEORGIA PEACH COBBLER

FOR THE FRUIT LAYER

Butter, for the baking dish

6 ripe peaches, peeled, pitted, and thinly sliced

⅓ cup (75 g) packed brown sugar

2 teaspoons fresh lemon juice

1½ teaspoons cornstarch

½ teaspoon vanilla extract

½ teaspoon ground cinnamon

Pinch ground nutmeg

Pinch ground ginger

TO MAKE THE FRUIT LAYER

1. Preheat the oven to 400°F (204°C, or gas mark 6).
2. Lightly coat a 2-quart (2 L) baking dish with butter. Add the peaches, brown sugar, lemon juice, cornstarch, vanilla, cinnamon, nutmeg, and ginger and toss to coat and combine.
3. Bake for 10 minutes to soften.

TO MAKE THE TOPPING

4. In a medium bowl, whisk the flour, brown sugar, baking powder, and salt until blended.
5. Using a pastry blender or your fingers, cut in or rub the butter until the mixture resembles coarse meal. Add the boiling water and toss just until combined.
6. In a small bowl, stir together the sugar and cinnamon until combined.
7. Remove the peaches from the oven. Using a tablespoon, drop the topping over the fruit. Sprinkle the cinnamon sugar over the topping and exposed filling.
8. Bake for 25 to 35 minutes until the fruit is bubbly and the topping is golden.
9. Serve warm.

FOR THE TOPPING

¾ cup (90 g) all-purpose flour

⅓ cup (75 g) packed brown sugar

¾ teaspoon baking powder

¼ teaspoon salt

5 tablespoons (70 g) butter, chilled and diced

3 tablespoons (45 ml) boiling water

2 tablespoons (25 g) granulated sugar

¾ teaspoon ground cinnamon

YIELD: SERVES 8

PREP TIME: 20 MINUTES

COOK TIME: 40 MINUTES

Sweet potato pie—kind of rolls off the tongue, doesn't it? Once you try this warm spiced beauty, ordinary pumpkin pie will be forever put aside. I love this pie topped with candied pecans or a fluffy scoop of maple-sweetened whipped cream.

SWEET POTATO PIE

1 (9-inch, or 23 cm) unbaked piecrust (store-bought or homemade)

2 cups (400 g) mashed sweet potatoes (about 2 medium)

1 cup (240 ml) milk, at room temperature

1 cup (200 g) sugar

¼ cup (60 ml) melted butter

2 large eggs, at room temperature

1½ teaspoons vanilla extract

½ teaspoon ground cinnamon

¼ teaspoon ground ginger

¼ teaspoon sea salt

⅛ teaspoon ground nutmeg

1. Preheat the oven to 350°F (177°C, or gas mark 4).
2. Fit the crust into a 9-inch (23 cm) pie pan.
3. In a large bowl, using an electric mixer, beat the sweet potato, milk, sugar, melted butter, eggs, vanilla, cinnamon, ginger, salt, and nutmeg until very smooth, stopping to scrape down the sides of the bowl with a spatula several times. Pour the filling into the piecrust.
4. Bake for 35 to 40 minutes until a knife inserted into the center of the pie comes out clean.
5. Cool the pie on a wire rack to room temperature before serving.

Adding soda pop to cake is inspiring—the taste is intense, and the carbonation acts as a leavener, which is why you omit the baking soda and baking powder in this recipe. This old-fashioned Southern creation graces tables at potlucks and church picnics and is common as the finish to a family barbecue dinner.

YIELD: SERVES 8

PREP TIME: 15 MINUTES

COOK TIME: 1 HOUR

7UP CAKE

TO MAKE THE CAKE

1. Preheat the oven to 325°F (163°C, or gas mark 3). Coat a 10-inch (30 cm) Bundt pan with cooking spray and dust it with flour, knocking out the excess.
2. In a large bowl, combine the butter and granulated sugar. Using an electric mixer, beat for about 5 minutes until very fluffy.
3. One at a time, add the eggs, beating well after each addition, and stopping to scrape down the sides of the bowl with a spatula after each, until very smooth.
4. Add the lime zest, lime juice, and vanilla and beat to combine.
5. Add the flour in five additions, alternating with the 7UP, beginning and ending with the flour, and beating until well combined. Pour the batter into the prepared Bundt pan.
6. Bake for about 1 hour until a toothpick inserted into the center of the cake comes out clean.
7. Let the cake cool for 10 minutes, then invert it onto a serving plate.

TO MAKE THE GLAZE

8. In a medium bowl, whisk the confectioners' sugar, milk, and lemon juice until very smooth. Drizzle the glaze over the cooled cake and serve.

FOR THE CAKE

Nonstick cooking spray

3 cups (360 g) cake flour, plus more for the pan

1½ cups (3 sticks, or 339 g) butter, at room temperature

2¾ cups (550 g) granulated sugar

5 large eggs, at room temperature

Grated zest of 1 lime

Juice of 1 lime

1½ teaspoons vanilla extract

¾ cup (180 ml) 7UP at room temperature

FOR THE GLAZE

2 cups (224 g) confectioners' sugar

¼ cup (60 ml) milk, at room temperature

1 tablespoon (15 ml) fresh lemon juice

SAUCES AND RUBS

SPICY

SWEET

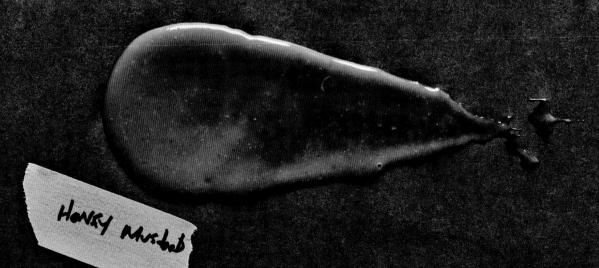

Honey Mustard

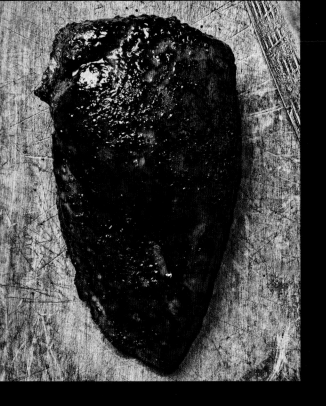

LET'S GET SOMETHING STRAIGHT:

You don't need to sauce your smoked meats and poultry to make them delicious. Sauces, mops, rubs, and marinades enhance the already-mouthwatering barbecue. That said, these are some of my favorites if you happen to want to add them to your meats. You will find classic tomato-based sauces, traditional Southern or Carolina-style vinegar sauces, and recipes inspired by sweet blueberries and watermelon. Mix and match the sauces with proteins in the book to your heart's content. For food-safety reasons, make sure that any sauce you will be using on raw or partially cooked meats is kept in a separate bowl (with separate brush or spoon) from sauce that you will be serving at the table.

Everyone needs a versatile barbecue sauce—use as a baste while cooking, brine or marinade before cooking, mop while smoking, apply after cooking, or serve on the side for dipping—to whip up when guests are on the way, or even just for everyday meals to make them more special. Mine is this easy recipe, which uses two sweeteners—brown sugar and honey—to create a complex, rich taste. Try this sauce on ribs, chicken, or mixed into juicy pulled pork.

SWEET BARBECUE SAUCE

1 cup (240 g) ketchup

2 tablespoons (30 g) brown sugar

1 tablespoon (15 ml) soy sauce

1 tablespoon (15 ml) Worcestershire sauce

1½ teaspoons honey

1½ teaspoons kosher salt

1½ teaspoons freshly ground black pepper

1½ teaspoons liquid smoke

1. In a medium saucepan, stir together the ketchup, brown sugar, soy sauce, Worcestershire sauce, honey, salt, pepper, and liquid smoke. Bring to a boil, stirring occasionally.
2. Turn the heat to low and simmer the sauce for 30 minutes, stirring occasionally, until the sauce has thickened.
3. Use immediately, or refrigerate in an airtight container for up to 1 month.

Like a little heat with your barbecue? Cayenne pepper and fresh jalapeño jazz up this tomato-based sauce with layers of flavor. You can adjust the quantities to suit your palate and use hotter peppers, such as habanero or serrano, if that's your thing. Try this sauce on any meat you want to smoke.

YIELD: MAKES ABOUT 1 CUP (ABOUT 250 G)

PREP TIME: 10 MINUTES

COOK TIME: 35 MINUTES

SPICY BARBECUE SAUCE

1. In a medium saucepan, stir together the ketchup, brown sugar, soy sauce, Worcestershire sauce, salt, black pepper, liquid smoke, cayenne, and jalapeño. Bring to a boil, stirring occasionally.
2. Turn the heat to low and simmer the sauce for 30 minutes, stirring occasionally, until the sauce has thickened.
3. Use immediately, or refrigerate in an airtight container for up to 1 month.

1 cup (240 g) ketchup

2 tablespoons (30 g) brown sugar

1 tablespoon (15 ml) soy sauce

1 tablespoon (15 ml) Worcestershire sauce

1½ teaspoons kosher salt

1½ teaspoons freshly ground black pepper

1½ teaspoons liquid smoke

1 teaspoon cayenne pepper

1 jalapeño pepper, seeded and minced

Honey and mustard are often combined in recipes because the sweet and slightly hot tastes balance each other perfectly. Plain yellow ballpark mustard is transformed here into a sauce that is so delicious, you might end up eating it with a spoon (I won't tell). Try a generous dollop on Hot Links from Scratch (page 69) in a soft bun or any cut of pork you like.

HONEY MUSTARD BARBECUE SAUCE

1 cup (176 g) yellow mustard

¾ cup (180 ml) apple cider vinegar

1 tablespoon (15 g) brown sugar

1 tablespoon (12.5 g) granulated sugar

1 tablespoon (18 g) kosher salt

1 tablespoon (6 g) freshly ground black pepper

1½ teaspoons liquid smoke

1½ teaspoons soy sauce

1½ teaspoons onion powder

1. In a medium saucepan, stir together the mustard, vinegar, brown sugar, granulated sugar, salt, pepper, liquid smoke, soy sauce, and onion powder. Bring to a boil, stirring occasionally.
2. Turn the heat to low and simmer the sauce for 30 minutes, stirring occasionally, until the sauce has thickened.
3. Use immediately, or refrigerate in an airtight container for up to 1 month.

If you are from the Carolinas, you probably grew up with this vinegar sauce paired with succulent pulled pork—one is rarely served there without the other. Because you can put this sauce together quickly with ingredients you probably have in your pantry, there is no reason to ever run out. Ever.

YIELD: MAKES ABOUT 1 CUP (240 ML)

PREP TIME: 10 MINUTES

COOK TIME: 35 MINUTES

VINEGAR SAUCE

1. In a medium saucepan, stir together the vinegar, honey, brown sugar, ketchup, red pepper flakes, and salt. Bring to a boil, stirring occasionally.
2. Turn the heat to low and simmer the sauce for 30 minutes, stirring occasionally, until the sauce has thickened.
3. Use immediately, or refrigerate in a sealed Mason jar for up to 1 month.

2 cups (480 ml) apple cider vinegar

¼ cup (80 g) honey

2 tablespoons (30 g) brown sugar

1½ teaspoons ketchup

1½ teaspoons red pepper flakes

1 teaspoon kosher salt

Instead of vinegar, this thick, sticky sauce gets its kick from bourbon. For a classic sauce with Kentucky roots, use dark molasses in place of the honey. This recipe works well with any type of barbecue, and I love it in baked beans, too.

BOURBON SAUCE

1 cup (240 g) ketchup

½ cup (120 ml) bourbon

2 tablespoons (30 g) brown sugar

1 tablespoon (15 ml) Worcestershire sauce

1½ teaspoons honey

1½ teaspoons kosher salt

1½ teaspoons freshly ground black pepper

1½ teaspoons liquid smoke

1. In a medium saucepan, stir together the ketchup, bourbon, brown sugar, Worcestershire sauce, honey, salt, pepper, and liquid smoke. Bring to a boil, stirring occasionally.
2. Turn the heat to low and simmer the sauce for 30 minutes, stirring occasionally, until the sauce has thickened.
3. Use immediately, or refrigerate in an airtight container for up to 1 month.

Blueberries in barbecue sauce? Certainly! The natural sweetness of the berries is the ideal complement to the umami flavor of soy sauce. If you don't have time to supervise this sauce on the stovetop, double the ingredients, throw them into a slow cooker, mash gently with a potato masher to crush the berries, and cook, covered, on low heat for 6 hours.

YIELD: MAKES ABOUT 1 CUP (ABOUT 250 G)

PREP TIME: 10 MINUTES

COOK TIME: 35 MINUTES

BLUEBERRY SAUCE

1. In a medium saucepan, stir together the blueberries, ketchup, vinegar, salt, pepper, honey, soy sauce, and liquid smoke. Bring to a boil, stirring occasionally.
2. Turn the heat to low and simmer the sauce for 30 minutes, stirring occasionally, until the sauce has thickened.
3. Use immediately, or refrigerate in an airtight container for up to 1 month.

2 cups (290 g) fresh blueberries

1 cup (240 g) ketchup

½ cup (120 ml) apple cider vinegar

1 tablespoon (18 g) kosher salt

1 tablespoon (6 g) freshly ground black pepper

1 tablespoon (20 g) honey

1½ teaspoons soy sauce

1½ teaspoons liquid smoke

YIELD: MAKES 2 CUPS
(ABOUT 500 G)

PREP TIME: 20 MINUTES

COOK TIME: 20 MINUTES

Believe it or not, watermelon is a common addition to barbecue sauces—it produces a refreshing, sweet, tangy sauce that is spectacular on ribs and with pulled pork. I think the best part of making this sauce is the leftover watermelon you can serve in thick wedges for dessert!

WATERMELON SAUCE

4 cups (600 g) chopped watermelon

1 cup (240 ml) water

¼ cup (60 ml) liquid smoke

1 tablespoon (15 g) brown sugar

1 tablespoon (18 g) kosher salt

1 tablespoon 6 g) freshly ground black pepper

1½ teaspoons soy sauce

1½ teaspoons onion powder

1. In a blender or food processor, purée the watermelon, then drain it through a fine-mesh sieve or cheesecloth set over a bowl to remove any larger pieces that remain.
2. In a medium saucepan, combine the drained watermelon, water, liquid smoke, brown sugar, salt, pepper, soy sauce, and onion powder. Bring to a boil over medium heat, stirring occasionally.
3. Turn the heat to low and simmer the sauce for 15 minutes, stirring occasionally, until the sugar is fully dissolved and the sauce has thickened.
4. Use immediately, or refrigerate in an airtight container for up to 1 month.

Mop, or sop as it is sometimes called, is used to infuse moisture and flavor into meat. You can even find specialized kitchen tools designed to apply this sauce to the meat, and they look just like miniature mops! This mop flavors our Whole Hog (page 125) but is good for any type of meat.

YIELD: MAKES ABOUT 1 CUP (240 ML)

PREP TIME: 10 MINUTES

COOK TIME: 30 MINUTES

HOG MOP

1. Preheat the oven to 400°F (204°C, or gas mark 6). Line a pie plate with aluminum foil.
2. Place the onion and garlic on the foil, drizzle them with the oil, and fold the foil over to form a loose packet. Roast for about 30 minutes until the vegetables are tender.
3. Transfer the onion and garlic to a blender and add the vinegar, salt, pepper, and paprika. Blend until very smooth.
4. Use immediately, or refrigerate in an airtight container for up to 1 month.

1 large onion, peeled and cut into eighths

1 garlic clove, peeled

1 teaspoon olive oil

¾ cup (180 ml) apple cider vinegar

1 tablespoon (18 g) kosher salt

1 tablespoon (6 g) freshly ground black pepper

1 tablespoon (8 g) paprika

This tart-sweet sauce is a beautiful addition to smoked meats—I especially like it as a side with pork or poultry. Don't worry if you think the texture is too thin after the sauce is finished; it will thicken as it cools.

CRANBERRY SAUCE

1 cup (200 g) sugar

¾ cup (180 ml) water

4 cups (400 g) fresh cranberries, rinsed and picked over

½ teaspoon ground cinnamon (optional)

½ teaspoon ground nutmeg (optional)

1 tablespoon (6 g) grated orange zest (optional)

1. In a large saucepan over high heat, stir together the sugar and water and bring to a boil. Reduce the heat to medium and simmer for about 2 minutes, constantly stirring, until the sugar dissolves.
2. Add the cranberries, cinnamon (if using), nutmeg (if using), and orange zest (if using) and bring the mixture back to a boil.
3. Turn the heat to low and simmer the sauce for about 10 minutes until most of the cranberries have burst.
4. Let the sauce cool completely to room temperature. Refrigerate the sauce in an airtight container for up to 1 week.

YIELD: MAKES ABOUT ¾ CUP (ABOUT 150 G)

PREP TIME: 5 MINUTES

HORN RUB

1. Add all of the ingredients to a bowl and stir them together thoroughly with a whisk, fork, or spoon.
2. When ready to use, rub ample amounts of the rub onto the surface of the meat, rubbing and pushing firmly to fill any crevices or pores and to ensure the rub adheres to the meat.
3. Use immediately or store in an airtight container in a cool, shady place for up to 6 months.

4 tablespoons (60 g) dark brown sugar

2 tablespoons (36 g) coarse salt

1 tablespoon (6 g) coarse black pepper

2 teaspoons garlic powder

2 teaspoons onion powder

1 teaspoon paprika

1 teaspoon cayenne pepper

ABOUT THE AUTHOR

Matt Horn, the chef and owner of Horn Barbecue in Oakland, California, is one of the most important figures in barbecue today. Matt grew up in the agricultural breadbasket of North America, in Fresno in California's Central Valley, where he built his own smokers from discarded oil barrels and abandoned propane tanks. He has continued to soak up barbecue wisdom from a wide variety of sources, from parents and grandparents to the most renowned pitmasters in the country, ever since then, perfecting his craft at each step of the way. He has been honored as one of *Food & Wine* magazine's "Best New Chefs in America," and his restaurant has been named one of *Esquire* magazine's "Best New Restaurants in America" and has earned earned the "Bib Gourmand" and "New Discovery" designations from Michelin. Matt tells the story of his decision to devote his life and career to barbecue—the daunting challenges he faced, the long hours he toiled, the hard-won lessons he learned—in the introduction to this book, where he reveals how his devotion to family and his commitment to honor the many great but unheralded Black pitmasters in U.S. history together have motivated him to succeed. His unique "West Coast Barbecue" style has earned hundreds of accolades from the *New York Times*, *Sunset* magazine, *Forbes*, the *San Francisco Chronicle*, and other outlets. His charitable arm, the Horn Initiative, has provided thousands of free meals to those in need in and around Oakland. He lives with his wife, daughter, and son in the San Francisco Bay Area.

INDEX